Festive

An Anthology of Award Winning Kannda Stories

Editor

Keshava Malagi

VEERALOKA

VEERALOKA BOOKS PVT. LTD.
207, 2nd Floor, 3rd Main, Chamarajpet
Bengaluru-560018. Mobile: 7022122121
E-mail: veeralokabooks@gmail.com
Website: www.veeralokabooks.com

KATHA SANKRANTI
An Anthology of Award Winning Kannda Stories
Edited by **Keshava Malagi**

Published by:
VEERALOKA BOOKS PVT. LTD.
207, 2nd Floor, 3rd Main
Chamarajpet, Bengaluru-560018

Mobile: +91 7022122121
E-mail: veeralokabooks@gmail.com
Website: www.veeralokabooks.com

Price: Rs. 249/-
Pages: 124
First Impression: March 2024

Paper used: 70 GSM NS Maplitho
Book size: 1/8th Demy

ISBN: 978-93-94942-92-9

VEERALOKA crew

Anand Rach
Anantha Kunigal
RajVishnu
Govind Vishnu
Vishwajith
Mamatha
Parvathi
Punith

Cover page illustration by:
Kiran Madalu

Inner pages design by:
Guruprasad

Editor's Note

The history of modern Kannada short stories is both rich and fascinating, dating back to the early 1900s. It was during this time that **Panje Mangesh Rao,** a pioneering figure in the Indian Renaissance, published a short story in *Suvasini,* a magazine, paving the way for modern Kannada short stories. **Keruru Vasudevachar,** an early and prolific writer, also made significant contributions to the genre.

While some experts and intellectuals argue that the origins of modern Kannada short stories can be traced to ancient *Jataka* tales, Shivakotiachary's *Vaddaradhane*, and other ancient narratives, others acknowledge the impact of "World Literature", a coinage of *Goethe*, on writers during the Indian Renaissance. This combination of local and global influences has allowed Kannada short stories to flourish, with authors exploring various themes and issues. Changes in perspectives, socio-political-economic issues, and emerging topics like individual identity, feminism, and the rise of Dalit and Other Backward Class consciousness have greatly influenced Kannada short story writing over the decades.

The support of little magazines, literary supplements, and other publications such as monthlies and fortnightlies have played a crucial role in the growth of Kannada short stories. The conciseness of poetry, the lyrical quality of an essay, and the expansiveness of a novel have all contributed to the evolution of the genre.

Publications organizing short story competitions have played a significant role in bringing forth high-quality stories and promoting emerging writers. Also, these competitions have a rich legacy of over eight decades and have recognized today's renowned writers like U R Anantha Murthy, P Lankesh, Poornachandra Tejaswi, Srikrishna Alanahalli, Besagarahalli Ramanna, Mogalli Ganesh, Vivek Shanbhag, Nataraj Huliyar, among others. These competitions have undoubtedly proved to be a springboard for many aspiring young writers to showcase their talent and achieve recognition.

Festive- Kathasankranti-2024 was a competition, truly exceptional in every way. From the Caliber of its participants to the innovation of its rules, it stands out as a true testament to excellence and creativity.

The significant literary event was organized by Veeraloka Publications.

The salient features of Kathasankranti-2024 were:

- To encourage new writers, only those without published anthologies were allowed to participate and the word limit of a story was increased to 3000.
- Prize money for first, second, and third winners was raised to 55,000, 30,000, and 20,000 (INR) correspondingly.
- The most captivating aspect for all participants in the competition was the translation of the award-winning stories into English, Telugu, and Malayalam languages, and the selection of seven stories handpicked by the juries and publishing them in the anthologies form.

We have selected ten stories for awards, translations, and publication in anthologies after months of robust processes.

The stories in this anthology exhibit exceptional style, language usage, narration, and innovative approaches toward the subject and theme.

The stories cover a wide range of themes, including the human experience of suffering, the complexities of life, and how people confront them through meditative efforts and understanding.

While reading these stories, readers may be confronted with issues such as identity, empathy, harmony, hypocrisy, confession, and creativity.

I thank all translators who made it possible to reach a larger reader base in Kannada, English, Telugu, and Malayalam-speaking communities. I must also thank Veerakaputra Srinivas, who organized the Kathasankranti-2024 and is now publishing in all languages mentioned earlier. The success of the spectacular event has happened with his support and cooperation.

Keshava Malagi
Editor
Bengaluru

Publisher's Note

Editor Keshav Malagi has already outlined the stories and judges' remarks. Rather than elaborating at length, allow me to succinctly articulate the purpose of Katha Sankranthi. The Kannada literary domain has been under the mistaken impression that readership is lacking. This perception mirrors a misstep seen in the Kannada film industry, which limited its reach by making assumptions about audience preferences in various regions like Kolar, Bellary, and Bidar. Similarly, the literary world has succumbed to a self-fulfilling prophecy by stating there are few readers, resulting in a focus on producing books solely for libraries. Consequently, vital information about new releases, noteworthy titles, and recommended reads has been withheld from readers, thus stifling innovation and transforming literature into a mere social service endeavor. Veeraloka stands out for its dedicated efforts to revitalize the stagnant literary landscape through innovative initiatives, among which Katha Sankranthi prominently features.

Rather than stating that there is a lack of readers for Kannada books, the Katha Sankranti initiative aims to broaden our market by translating Kannada literature into other languages, thereby increasing its readership. Renowned storyteller Keshav Malagi leads this endeavor and has introduced new regulations for the storytelling competition, resulting in emerging storytellers claiming victory. I have immense confidence in our writers' narratives, leading us to venture into translating these tales into various languages. It is with great pride that we introduce the concept of Pan India, traditionally associated with the realm of cinema, into Kannada literature through Veeraloka. The stories within are certain to captivate your interest.

You may experience the joy of reading.

Veerakaputra Srinivas
Publisher, Veeraloka Books

Content

Keshava Malagi (1963), is an important Kannada writer who has created a niché in short stories.

He has published five collections of stories, two novels, and two essay collections.

Malagi is also known for his translation contributions and readers. He has published French and African literature, Gabriel García Márquez in Kannada. He also has translated Medieval Bhakti-Sufi poets, Kabir.

Malagi has three decades of professional experience working in media, publication, social development, and teaching. He has three academy awards and a fellowship to his credit.

1

Kirabunkal

Ravikumar Neeha

Translated by **Shashikumar**

'If I snatch it from you, why do you behave as though someone has stuck a rod up your ass? Why do you seem so lost in such bullshit thoughts? Screw your stupid face! You fuck around aimlessly without any thoughts of your home or wife. There isn't anyone to tell you what to do. Don't they say anything to you? Those who tell you what to do are themselves lousy bastards. Your father ditched you here with me and disappeared. I'm working my ass off just to take care of you. I don't want to live this dirt poor life anymore, I'm not hanging around to watch your antics much longer…

Seena was enjoying watching reels of beautiful girls and couples on his mobile. He thought to himself, 'Look at these people, they're so attractive.'

Seena stared at his phone awestruck. He watched pretty faces to distract himself from his ugly and dark-skinned wife. 'Why did I marry this snub-nosed female? I see only pretty faces here. It must be my mother's revenge, which trapped me in this goddamn pigsty. Had I married one of these chicks, how nice that would've been. They're swinging their hips and winking, waving their hands. Wow! I got married when I was still unaware of all this. If I'd the chance now, I'd remarry someone from here.'

How would Seena, lost in his world of eye-catching reels and sexy girls, heed the words of his mother, Eeri?

Shalini was not the only one who was unattractive. Even Seena, when he attained that age, came to know how dark he was. He tried to fix his looks by constantly washing his face three to four times a day with Lux soap. As he saw in the ads on TV, he switched from Lux to Santoor to Pears to Dove; he had turned his face into a science lab. He would curse his dark complexion whenever he saw fair people, 'All these people have become so fair by washing their faces nonstop, why've I been born like this?'

As his mustache hairs started to pop up, Seena's face darkened even more. In spite of all his attempts, he did not become any fairer but he did not stop trying to lighten his features.

Seena, alias Sreenivasa, was the one and only son of Eeri and Mudli. Seena was not the type of son born through years of prayer and sacrifice. He would have come along regardless of any such trials and tribulations. Watching those religious, god-fearing people who made sacrifices and offerings to the gods in the hope of children, Mudli would exclaim, 'You don't need all these to birth children, just a strong push! What the fuck do these guys think they're doing? In this village filled with people, would none show up for a good dick?'

Eeri was very fair-skinned. She acted as a talisman to ward off evil spirits for the entire household. She was round-faced and had a busty chest; a feast for the eyes of the entire village. When she woke up at sunrise to clean the front yard, she would hike her saree up around her waist causing people's hearts to thump with excitement. Her beauty messed with the minds of the people in the village and favored the entire village. Mudli was like a virile tool that impregnated women at a single glance. He was not the sort to sit still with just one child. If he had remained alive, he would have caused Eeri's lap to overflow with at least five children. But what happened that day was like a bolt out of the blue.

That night, the night of the new moon, it was as dark as a bear's ass. One could not see the face of their neighbor. On this night, when the land slept in darkness as though blanketed with the dark, Mudli was walking towards *Kirabunkal* after a search for Seena. At that moment, there was a sound in the air as though of a person in pain. Although one could hear the person, there was nothing to be seen. Mudli moved towards the sound. As he walked, Mudli got lost in the darkness. No one ever found out what happened to Mudli as he walked towards the strange sound. When morning came, Mudli lay collapsed in a pit outside Chandranna's farm. It had been quite a while since he breathed his last.

2

A long time had passed since the events of that night. People had drawn many breaths in the intervening time. Taletellers and those who enjoyed listening to them had long since disappeared. It had been years since tales were born and created. Earlier, when Mappurajja, Sanrangi, and Hirnagira had still been alive, there was no dearth of tales. The tales of this village and those adjoining it, the tale of Rama-Lachmana, the tale of Konti's birthing children who did not belong to her husband, this fort of tales that had been built around the village took years to circulate the village, changing the airs and features of these tales. It was impossible to differentiate tales belonging to this village from those of the next. Newcomers were often included in the village tales, and dropped at will once people lost interest in them. Tales were intertwined to create new ones, and roamed freely all over the village.

One such tale, having perambulated the entirety of the village a multitude of times, now rested in the same household for the last nine years. Similarly, there were more than a hundred such tales in each household. Each such tale had generated children, grandchildren, and great-grandchildren, and formed a dynasty of their own. These tales had become a family. The forefathers would leave these tales untouched, allowing them to live a life of their own.

However, in recent times, there were no people to even ask the tales how they were doing. In any village, no one would pay heed to one, having neither time nor ear to lend to tales. People were busy on their phones or watching TV. The tales started feeling like their lifetime was coming to an end. The tales, which used to entertain, started feeling boredom themselves. When people faced suffering, they would sit the tales by their side and tell them of their troubled lives. This would cause their pains and sorrows to vanish into thin air. But now, the tales found it difficult to even breathe. Where were the gods that breathed life into these tales? Tales were forced to leave their habitats and step outside. Were they bound to their homes? There must be more like them in other homes too. So thinking, the tales searched the nooks and crannies of the village and looked for other such tales in the homes of other religions and castes. But there was not a single tale remaining that lived a life of untroubled ease. None of the tales had any living thing remaining to listen to them.

Hirikateyajji, grandmother to the tales, was on the last threshold of her life and was very troubled by the times that had come to pass. She sent a message to all the tales calling for a meeting. The tale that had not seen daylight and sat in a hut, the tale which sat on a colorful mat, the tale of the full night, Kuntasenniga's tale, the tales of animals, birds, humans, and all other living beings, all these tales left their homes and came out.

The Brahmanical *Puranapunya* tales wondered whether they too should join the others; they were skeptical of entering the homes of the lower caste tales and being touched by them. They might be polluted by them, and this fear of desecration kept them in their own homes. Where would they go to feel remorse if they were touched by others? They thought to themselves over and over, 'We'll be written anyway, there are so many to write. So why must we join the other tales?'

When they realized that all the other tales from the households of different castes would be going, they decided to go. They planned to wear white *dhotra* and draw a *nama* on their foreheads. They thought, 'We'll maintain a distance and keep from touching anyone. Let's go and see what happens.'

It was a strange night, eerily silent and calm. One could not see the face of another. All the tales started gathering around the *Jagtikatte*, the peepal tree central to the village. *Hirikateyajji* had worked hard for this. She was a tale that would not end even in a year. Her tale was of considerable significance to the village. In their younger days, the great tales would not end even in a decade or a generation. But, *Hirikateyajji* was a tale that would last for hardly a year. The major hindrance this tale faced was, 'My tale is at an end. If my clan does not grow, will this world remain? I've caused the end to this world. Therefore, I'll have to find a solution. The fort of tales must grow.'

Having said this, she passed on the responsibility to handle this propagation to a tale that would take less than a week to end. The chosen tale, *Three Night Tale*, had also realized that the age of tales would end within their lifetime. He decided, 'Let people say what they want.'

He did not pay any heed to the words of others, and informed every house of how things stood, 'This is how it is.'

The tales that had forgotten how to speak, and the tales that could not see, and the tales that could not walk, all felt energized.

The *Three Night Tale* pondered upon whether or not to invite the *Puranapunya* tales. The tale took a couple of days to reach a decision. When everyone slept, the tale stood at the doorway of the *Puranapunya* tales and apprised them of the current state of affairs, 'This is how it is.'

Perturbed by the unexpected visit, the *Puranapunya* tales said, 'Aiyoh! Why don't you just leave? Have you got nothing else to do? We're continually birthing new tales. Even if they might be illegitimate children, we're constantly adding new members to our family.'

Although they had hastily sent the *Three Night Tale* away, in their hearts they were not quite happy with themselves.

The *Three Night Tale* returned, relieved by the fact that it had informed all the streets about the current state of events. The tales that were coming from different lanes and alleys were also joining in with the hope of survival. This meeting was the only means for continuing their existence. As all these tales gathered around the peepal tree, the *Jagtikatte* became a bustling village.

3

Mudli was the most handsome man in the entire village. His son was Seena. As Seena was moving towards adulthood, he was looking for a chance to become more manly. It was then that he found Vimli. She had just attained puberty and had recently begun experiencing strange desires in her dreams. She spent many sleepless, restless nights until she met Seena. They both felt attracted to each other and started meeting at *Kirabunkal*, outside the village. They began spending time with each other, chitchatting and exploring each other's bodies. Vimli felt Seena was her sweetheart, and Seena felt the same.

How long could this continue without people noticing? When the whole world was suffering, for these two, staying apart for even a minute felt like hell. They would meet in private, away from the prying eyes of the villagers. During this affair, Vimli's father Chandranna noticed something strange in her behavior. Following her movements outside the house, he happened to witness Vimli and Seena's flirting. How could he remain quiet? He screamed at them. Vimli was shivering in fear and begged him to forgive them. Chandranna thrashed Seena, beating him almost to death. He said to Seena, 'I won't let you get away with this,' as he dragged Vimli away from Seena.

In that dark night, none could notice what became of Seena. Blood flowed from his body, and he became numb with pain. He felt like the life was draining out of him. He lay collapsed upon the ground like a dead tree.

Like every night, Mudli exited his home to urinate. He returned to his home and laid himself upon the mat to sleep. Seena, who had slept next to him that night, was not to be seen on the mat. He wondered where Seena could have gone. Did he leave the house? Did he go outside to defecate? He was nowhere to be seen for quite a long while. Where did he disappear? So, Mudli left the house in search of Seena. He could not find him anywhere in that dark, silent night. He walked straight towards the *Jagtikatte* and came out of the village to *Kirabunkal.* He found his son, Seena, in an unconscious state. Blood and spittle poured from his mouth. Mudli slowly picked him up and held him, walking him back towards the hut.

At home Eeri was chewing betelnut, wondering where her husband and son could have gone. She was shocked to see her son in this state, 'What happened to him? Why is he like this? Oh my god!'

She helped him drink water and then went outside to prepare some herbal medicine. She dressed his wounds. After he could breathe once again, Mudli asked Seena , 'What happened to you, son? Why were you lying there?'

Seena took an hour to say, '*Ki......ra......bun....kal.*'

Mudli snapped the towel at his shoulder and decided that he would go immediately and find out what had taken place. He came to *Kirabunkal* but could not find anything. All that could be seen were some holes in the ground where the channel had eroded the soil. He was clueless as to why his son had happened to be lying here in his current state. Soon, some people in the distance could be heard exclaiming, 'Look at him, he's there, he's there!'

Mudli shouted, ' Who's that?'

Then, five or six people came towards Mudli and pounded him almost to death. He heard Chandranna's voice. He wanted to ask him, 'Why?', but his words remained in his mouth.

They had beaten him so badly that he could hardly speak. Mudli was unable to move his body any further. He lay down right there. The men who beat him said, 'Beat him so much that he won't smell anything foul.'

Their voices spread across the area and crossed *Kirabunkal*, reaching the *Jagtikatte*.

4

The tales gathered at the *Jagtikatte* had not met each other in a long time. All of them looked quite happy to be meeting one another. They reached out to touch and hug each other, exchanging greetings and pleasantries. Their happiness knew no bounds.

Hirikateyajji said, 'If it continues on like this, it'll be dawning soon. People in the area will start their morning activities. The reason for which we have gathered here won't be fulfilled, and we won't be able to meet like this anytime in the near future. We all also have our own work to get to. So, let's talk and figure out a way.'

'Listen, tales! We haven't been in touch with each other for the longest time. We don't even recall our own faces, so how could we recall each other's faces? It must be because of our good deeds from the past that we have met here like this. Let's not be content with just seeing each other. We still have life in us, our clan must propagate. Our plans haven't come to fruition. There aren't any more people around to tell tales. Although we're here to tell tales, there're no people to listen to us. If it continues like this, we can't survive. The land that has survived for hundreds of years, how'd it survive? And where'd this land get its life from? If we create tales, this land, this air, these trees, these plants, will all be happy and healthy. It seems that they're all coming to an end. How long can we hold our breaths? We're caught between life and death. If we think of dying and getting to heaven, what would become of the gift we have received from our ancestors? We'd be unsuccessful in spreading our tales. How long can we live like this?'

She gasped for breath and stopped talking.

Silence…silence…

Hirikateyajji's words caused their lives to pass in front of their eyes. *Puranapunya*, who had remained quiet all this while, started speaking, 'You're finished. None remain to listen to your tales, tell them, create them. That we can believe. But, we've a separate concern. By spreading lies, truth has been lost. *Puranapunya* tales used to live with great pride. But, that world remains no more. We've forgotten which tales belong to us, *Punya*, and which are made up. Each tale has been turned into a hundred new ones. TV is filled with tales composed of lies. When we were born, we were told that the tales we created would create life. There should be no deception or negativity in those tales. There are millions of lives that depend upon our tales. But, today, one man can't tolerate the tale of another. Other living things will never be able to enter the tales of people from today, but will remain in photos. We're tired of hearing false tales. Where's the end to all this?'

There was a commotion as the tales began discussing what had been said.

It was almost the time when the stone and the water melted. All the tales said to *Hirikateyajji* that she was the oldest person among them; she was their ancestor, and she had to tell them how to proceed. Everyone waited for *Hirikateyajji's* next words. At this moment, they glimpsed a human walking towards them. This caused a furore in the group as they felt a panic upon seeing him. The man did not look towards the *Jagtikatte*, but walked straight past.

Three Night Tale said, 'Look brothers, men used to give life to tales until now. From now on, we'll run the lives of men. We'll make tales about these men. We'll show them what we are capable of. Until they understand what we are, we'll continue to make these tales. Only then will men return to the straight path.'

This was the decision that the group agreed upon.

Hirikateyajji began, 'Look, this will create a further problem.'

Even then, what was to happen would come to pass.

5

… As all this was happening, it was unsure why, just before the death of Mudli, people began to drop to the ground like dried leaves. TV was constantly running news of speeding ambulances and sudden deaths. Anyone who coughed or even touched someone else would spread the disease. There was no cure. If anyone tried to run, they would be grabbed and made to stay in a closed room. These tales that spread caused a widespread panic. If anyone coughed or even looked unwell, they would be sequestered. The entire village quaked in fear of what could happen. Within this duration, Mudli passed away within a period of fifteen days. Whether Mudli died of the sickness or something else was unknown. But, he was no more.

The villagers began to tell Eeri that now that her husband was dead, the government would compensate her. They asked her to put in an application to the government. Eeri said, 'Mudli gave me Seena. Please show me a way to help him settle down in life. This'll relieve me of my responsibilities.'

The compensation that would materialize today or tomorrow never did come. The years passed in wait. She was exhausted from the upbringing of Seena. Seena was the only memory she had of Mudli.

Thinking that he was a fatherless child, Eeri brought Seena up with great love and affection. Mudli's passing had caused Seena's behavior to change. Since Seena's happiness was all that mattered to Eeri, she would give him whatever he wanted. Seena wanted a mobile, so Eeri bought him one. He watched girls on the mobile all day long. He would lie awake at night, watching whatever he wanted under the cover of his blanket. He would watch pornographic material and touch himself in the night, waking up clammy after his wet dreams. Sometimes, he would seem completely lost in his thoughts.

Mudli passed away mysteriously just like this. Sahukar Chandranna, the village chief, made it sound as though Mudli had some disease. He pretended that the sickness that befell the entire nation was the reason for Mudli's death. Mudli was bound up in five or six sarees and his wounds were covered up. An excavator was used to dig a hole as deep as the height of two persons, and Mudli was dropped into it. He was covered up in mud. Seena, who was lost in other thoughts, was made to handle the last rites.

Since then, Seena was not as he had been. He was always laughing, lost in his mobile. Thinking Seena could not remain like this, Eeri eventually found Shalini in the nearby village and got him married. Seena loved his phone even more than Shalini. If anyone was available to give him a meal, he would eat it, but if not, he was lost in his phone all day long. Seena remembered nothing of the wounds he had, what had happened to him, whether he had been possessed by a ghost or a spirit. An adult had become like a child in behavior. It was like a child who still played with toys had been expected to perform marital duties. Whatever he did with Shalini, he told the entire village, telling them about Shalini's body and their nightly activities. The entire village was titillated by this.

6

The tales, who had lost all their happiness, had begun to understand the world of the humans, 'We're starting to figure out what the world is like now. We'll make tales to mirror the world and its workings.'

So saying, they began the job of creating tales. These humans, who did not want instructive tales, would be given sensational tales instead. The tales changed their appearance to mimic what humans wanted now. They talked about male-female affairs, the clash between religions and communities, etc. When tales like these were being spread, what would become of the feelings of the soul? The tales cared nothing for what happened to humans. They created tales as they saw fit and spread them. Mudli's death laid the groundwork for the creation of tales such as these. A barren land, storieless, had been engulfed in rains and fecundity by the death of Mudli. Various tales were born upon this land.

One tale said,

'... If Mudli's body was lying at Sahukar Chandranna's farm, then he must have been murdered by Chandranna. His wife had been having an affair with Mudli. It had been going on for quite a while. When this tale fell on the ears of Chandranna, he gathered his men and waited for Mudli on the night of the new moon. They beat him to death...'

'Yes, possibly. Mudli was always at the house of Sahukar Chandranna. He behaved as though he was the owner of Chandranna's house. It's good that this happened to him.'

Then another responded,

'No, no, it wasn't like that. Sahukar Chandranna's daughter Vimli had recently reached puberty. Mudli showed her the ways of the amorous world. Due to this, Vimli's menstrual cycle was disrupted. Chandranna asked Vimli who could have done this, dismayed that this could have happened to his daughter. Then, he waited in the night to kill Mudli.'

A third piped up,

'Aiyoh! You all are unaware of the true tale. Sahukar Chandranna had an affair with Mudli's wife. They met on the night of every new moon. When he heard of what was going on, Mudli waited for the new moon and followed Chandranna. He fought with Sahukar, and that led to Mudli's death. Look at Mudli's son Seena, he looks as dark as Sahukar Chandranna.'

The tale, that had been born in a hurried moment, narrated this tale. Seena, who had looked like his father Mudli until then, now started looking like Sahukar. All the tales clasped their hands in surprise, and said 'Why did this never occur to us?'

All these colorful tales traveled across the village. They fell upon the ears of Eeri and then Seena. These tales shut the mouth of Eeri. The people started telling tales according to their own understanding and imagination. All humans wanted to satiate their internal desires. Because of these colorful tales, the men in the village were entertained. They imagined Eeri as they pleased.

According to the narration of these tales, Sahukar Chandranna's wife suddenly came over and slept with Mudli. Her daughter Vimli too was forced to sleep with Mudli. Mudli's wife Eeri too had to sleep with Chandranna. Those who had heard these tales imagined themselves in the place of Mudli, fantasizing about the happenings in the tales and being excited by them. These men had forgotten the faces of their own wives. In their minds, Sahukar Chandranna's wife, Eeri, and Vimli, were all that were to be seen.

If this was the case with the men in the village, the women had their own take on things, 'This shouldn't have happened to Eeri.'

They felt disturbed and anguished, 'If Eeri sleeps with Sahukar Chandranna, so be it. Why should these men care about it? If she sleeps with Sahukar Chandranna, would her private parts tear apart? It's her own wish to do as she pleases.'

They worried about Vimli. Where did she go? Is she even alive and breathing? Have they stopped her breath? These thoughts passed through their minds.

7

Hirikateyajji was fed up with all these words made up by the tales. She said, 'Who the hell did I give this responsibility to?!?! On top of everything else, humans are careless people who behave like drunken monkeys. If it continues like this, we'll be fucked! Isn't there any solution to this? *Kirabunkal* must show us the way.'

Hirikateyajji fastened her pouch to her waist and walked up to the gathering holding her walking stick, '*Kirabunkal*, which has been the progenitor of tales for generations, is now witnessing this. What has happened to you, *Kirabunkal*, the chieftain of the tales? Is this working out fine for you? Why're you disturbing us so much? You used to give birth to magnificent tales. I too was born of you. Where'd that love go? The people such as you, who used to manage the lives of the whole village, have become like this. Who'll take care of us now? Who'll we blame for our state? Why're you sulking so much? It's true that we no longer have the wherewithal to make good tales. We no longer have the imagination. That does not mean that we should be creating evil tales. We never resorted to that in the past. Now the village is overrun by bad tales. The true, good tales have become weak and feeble. Those tales are the ones that mean life to us and to the entire world. What must we do if you fall silent like this? All these years we've never come to you with our heads bowed like this. Now the time has come that we must beseech you. You have seen so many things in all these centuries. I too no longer have the lifeforce that I previously had. It's time for me to depart soon. Now you, and you alone, can find a way to save this world.'

Hirikateyajji's words touched the heart of *Kirabunkal.*

Kirabunkal finally spoke up, 'How're you, daughter? Once you left here, I never saw you again. It's only now that you're here. I've been here since the birth of this village. The trees, plants, animals, birds that lived and breathed all around me, where've they gone? They'd energy, but I've nothing. There's none to ask how I'm. I've nowhere to go. I'm so done with the people and the games they play. I'm tired of watching them. I've no one to turn to. No one that I can tell about my life and my feelings. Everyone has a life of their own. Why must elders live on in this state, Watching the lives of people who care not for us? My ribs and bones will crumble to dust and be blown away. Not just Mudli, but a lot of people have lost their lives and become skin and bones. They're buried in these streets. All that is left of them are their skeletons. As soon as I wake up everyday, I see one or another mishap. I've lived here for centuries, and it has now fallen to me to see the lifeless corpses of those I watched for ages. I provided fresh air and rainfall. I'm now a heap of cadavers. Those who fell in front of me, they've long since disintegrated into nothingness. What used to seem green and fresh, is now all bloody red. I no longer have any hopes or dreams in this life. My life can't lie in waiting for countless more corpses. So much has happened, and no one has seemed to care. Now, finally, you have come to ask me. Look at this village, it has become a godforsaken hellhole. These flesh and blood humans are chopping us into bits and disposing of us.'

Kirabunkal had spoken until she could speak no more. She fell into a silence.

After some time, she continued…

'Hmm, if people want the world to go on, they must unite and come together as one. If one becomes self-serving and thinks only of themselves, the world will fall apart like grains of salt. The air has become lifeless, the water bodies have dried up, our breaths no longer nourish us or give us energy. The people of this world have no ears to lend us. They all have a world of their own to inhabit. Everyone seems to think they live in a world of their own. Their universe is coming to an end, so they have resorted to living like this. Let us also see what we can do. We've to go forward with the situation at hand. No one knows when these bastards' lives will come to an end. If this were to pass, what would become of our lives? Let alone our lives, what'll happen to the lives of the humans?'

Hirikateyajji became very distressed at these words.

8

The agonized *Kirabunkal* used to be a wall that stood against all odds for the village that was full of life. It was the life and soul of the village. All lives eventually found their way into the shade of *Kirabunkal.* Time upon time, the rain, the wind, the sunlight, they all ran smoothly. The clouds would not even move without the consent of *Kirabunkal.* Even the sun would have to get *Kirabunkal's* permission to enter the village. Before this difficult time had befallen the village, *Kirabunkal* was like a protective barrier for the village. Nowadays, buildings were even built upon one another and then covered by factories. This caused *Kirabunkal* to melt and become powerless over time. Even today, *Kirabunkal's* only concern was the safety of the village. Day by day, these adverse explosions caused the tree to gradually collapse. Her chest cavity was falling in on itself, leaving it pockmarked with holes. *Kirabunkal* was trying to fight against these odds…

On the other hand, the tales in the village had consumed Mudli, Eeri, Sahukar Chandranna and Vimli, and were living a life of happiness. They brought discord among the classes. Seena was as he had been, and the village was living its daily life. Eeri waited for Seena to return to normalcy. Tales, in the name of love and honor, had caused the lives of the lower caste people to be lost. Video clips of girls peeing were being recorded and circulated. The entire world had been dragged into watching these kinds of videos, these kinds of tales. The humans of the world awaited such tales. Tales forgot food and water, and waited with baited breath. The village, the scabbed-over wound where tales used to be born once a day, now gave birth to three, from three to thirty, thirty to three hundred, three hundred to three thousand, and kept growing... Becoming the village full of false stories...

■

Ravikumar Neeha, winner of the first prize in the KathaSankranti-2024 competition, is a literary critic and research scholar and a native of Tumkur district. Ravikumar is a lecturer by profession. His recent publication `Arasu Kurangaraya' traces the history of a Dalit King who ruled a portion of Tumkur, which is very close to Bengaluru, the capital of modern Karnataka state.

Translator of this story **Shashikumar** is a research scholar and editor who is currently pursuing his PhD in Canada. Shashikumar has written critical essays and articles on language and literature.

2

Peanut Candy

ASG: Shashi Kumar

Translated by **Keshava Malagi**

When all the men and women of the village were busy in the kitchen, when the whole town was quiet mode, intermittent sounds would echo through the village. These were the voices and sounds of hairpin vendors, Ice candy, Oil, plastic vessel sellers, utensil sellers, mendicant fortune tellers, and bear players, and wandering alms mongers. They would shout with their peculiar voices and knock on doors and enquire whether anybody was interested in buying the stuff. Babu who was studying in the third standard was always fascinated by these voices. He would follow them and mimic their voices, but return home when they were scolded. He was obsessed with getting the item before his mother asked for it in exchange for fallen long hair.

He would receive a scolding from his mother for making this bargain for sure. To avoid getting scolded by his mother, Babu would sometimes efface long strands of hair from a neighbor's house! Occasionally, his mother would express her appreciation towards him for his actions. His father's wine bottles have often been used to get ice candy for him. He would collect Pongamia seeds to sell to oil extractors and make some extra cash to enjoy at the local fair. Babu had a business relationship with several small vendors, but he had a particularly close friendship with one vendor who was 35-40 years his senior, and a little taller. Although people referred to him as Mullasabi, Babu found it difficult to call his full name Mohammad Basheer, so he addressed him as Basheer. Basheer was the first Muslim person Babu had ever met. Brother Basheer wore a cap on his head, with a cloth ring on top, and carried a bamboo basket that was a little shorter than him. He would enter the village with a shout, "Peanut candy...peanut candy," wearing a long Kurta, loose pants, and sound-making slippers.

His voice would peak first, then the 'dy' letters would receive a peculiar stress. The sound of Basheer would alert the whole village, and Babu would hurry to Basheer. Even getting a penny at home was so difficult that elders would feel that they were giving away their entire savings! Although Basheer was generous enough to sell candy at a cheaper price, the village boys and Babu still felt like 'they could only buy peanut candy in their dreams.' When people buy candy, boys often stand with saliva in their mouths. Babu only tasted candy when buyers showed sympathy or Basheer shared leftovers. Babu followed Basheer like a tail, till the end of the sale in hopes of tasting some candy pieces.

One day, while following Basheer, Babu showed him his house when Basheer entered his street and asked if his house was on this street. Basheer placed the Bambu basket on the floor and asked the boy to fetch some drinking water for him. Babu wanted to have a detailed look at Basheer's basket. He asked his mother to get water for Basheer Anna and lifted the cloth ring, revealing hidden candy. When Mother arrived with water, Basheer engaged in a conversation with her. During their talk,

Basheer learned that Babu was a nickname and that the boy's real name was Shashikumar. Basheer jokingly invited Babu to come to his home with him, but Babu declined by shaking his head.

This is how Babu and Basheer's friendship developed. Babu would always be present in the village when Basheer visited, except on school days. They would walk around the village streets, conversing without concern for their age difference. Babu would talk about the happenings in school, and the festivals they celebrated, then, Basheer would share stories from other villages he visited. Regardless of whether the Peanut Candy were sold or not, Babu's share was always guaranteed. Villagers taunted him, "Your name matches his relationship. Pierce his Pajama, you two are meant for each other!" Babu would get upset and ask Basheer why only Muslims should be named Babu. Basheer used to respond with a laugh and give some kind of answer.

Excessive heat would cause Babu's nose to bleed. Despite treatments, it would abruptly reappear during summers. On occasion, gossipmongers spread false and harmful information to Babu's mother. You named your son with a Muslim name. Besides, your family consumes pork! That is the reason his nose bleeds! She considered the matter seriously and decided to stop cooking pork at home. She advised her son not to touch ham, explaining that it is considered sacred by some people, and bad for your name. During feasts, she made sure to keep a watchful eye on her son and prevent him from consuming ham.

●

On a Sunday, Dharmanna, a fellow villager, and rich farmer organized a feast to celebrate his brother's wedding. As a special treat for the guests, he prepared ham in addition to the chicken and mutton dishes. Babu and his friends thoroughly enjoyed the pork and returned home satisfied, falling asleep soon after. Slowly dark fell. Babu's mother noticed her son had a nosebleed when she switched on the light. It was a coincidence! She immediately poured water over Babu's head and washed his nose. While washing the dishes in the backyard, she suddenly remembered something and walked to Babu where he was sleeping, watching the light coming through the bulb.

"Did you eat ham?" She asked him. If he had said imminently "No" she would have believed. He gave a pause and replied: "No". She assumed that he had consumed ham, and took a stick resting in the corner of the foyer and bashed him. "I will never eat again", Babu begged.

She was angry and said, "I taught you like a parrot, yet you still ate ham with your filthy mouth". She later cried while sitting alone.

●

A week later, when Basheer visited the village, Babu asked him why he didn't eat ham. Basheer was concerned about how he would explain to the young boy that certain foods were not acceptable to different gods. He said, "Just as your gods do not accept certain foods, our God does not like pork." Though Babu was not satisfied with the answer, kept quiet. The punishment from his mother made him avoid pork.

One day, when Babu was with Basheer, some mischievous boys saw them and called out to them. Basheer bent down to lift the basket of candy from his head, hoping to sell them to some boys. The boys began to use abusive language to say filthy things to him suddenly. Basheer was deeply wounded by the sudden assault. His face lost all its color, turning completely pale. He grabbed the basket and walked away. Babu did not understand the undercurrent of the episode. He didn't speak but followed Basheer.

Basheer was too tired and sat on the bench of a bridge, where Babu joined him, waiting for Basheer to speak. "If I had grown up properly for my age, I would have given those boys a tough response today. Why was I cursed to be born like this?", Basheer thought to himself. Then he put his hand in the basket, grabbed some peanut candy offered them to Babu.

Babu had always aspired to this moment, but now he is not inclined to eat. He nodded his head and started walking towards home. Basheer also didn't feel like calling him. He walked towards the bus stand with tears in his eyes.

●

Basheer did not appear in the village after the bitter episode occurred. However, Babu kept waiting for him. Later a fortnight Babu became furious with those boys and cursed them. He went to his aunt's place for an occasion. While playing with his cousins, he heard the shrill voice: 'Peanut Candy'. Babu cheered up with a colorful face. Kids playing with him ran away from his response. Though Babu felt unusual, bothered a little. He was full of joy as he saw Basheer. The peanut vendor was also very happy as he met an old friend. Both sat on the bench under the Banyan tree. They spoke for hours.

When Basheer offered him candy, he refused by saying "Come to our village, then I will accept it", then went back to play with his pals. He asked his friends why did they ran away when they saw Peanut Candy Man. They said that he was a sorcerer. By offering sweets, he will take away the children and later tame them to listen to what he says. Babu was disgusted by that, withdrew from the game, went back home, and slept.

●

Maybe two weeks or so passed. This time Basheer visited Babu's village. Soon he heard the voice of candy man Babu somehow scared. He went home and never came outside. Basheer thought that Babu would have gone to relatives' place. Next time it did not happen again. Babu's doubts were cleared. Both were happy. They sat and spoke with an open heart. Basheer again offered him candy. Again, Babu's mind was occupied with words uttered by the boys of Aunt's village. Looking around, Babu asked him: "Will you eat half of it?" "I can, whenever I feel like eating!" Basheer's reply put Babu in suspense again.

"Do you kidnap children?" Suddenly Babu questioned Basheer.

Laughing aloud Basheer replied: "When children cry and when they are unbending their mothers tell them that. Why would I kidnap children?"

Unconvinced Babu wasn't ready to eat the sweet. Fed up with this Basheer opened the basket and put back the candy. Babu felt that his behavior was inappropriate. So, he followed Basheer. The stubborn candy vendor did not look back and walked. Meanwhile, the assailant boys took the weighing instrument from Basheer's basket. When Babu saw this mischief, he pulled Basheer's shirt and informed him. When Basheer turned back those boys were laughing. Basheer chased them with his basket. They were teasing and raging at him. Basheer started begging them to give back his balance. They refused to give the Balance and sat on a bench. Basheer sat next to them. Desperate Babu witnessed helplessly.

If Basheer offers candy in exchange for Balance, they would give Balance, the boys demanded. Hopeless Basheer tried to give them sweets. But unhappy boys put their hands into the basket, grabbed a handful of peanut candy, threw the Balance, and went away. Basheer was full of anger. He didn't bother the presence of Babu and walked away. Confused Babu followed him to the bus stop. Even then Basheer did not open his mouth. He boarded the bus. Babu came back home.

Basheer was perturbed by the boys' behavior and the humiliation he went through was hurting him badly. He decided not to visit the village again! It's firm! And he never came back. However, Babu always waited for him to come. Soon after summer vacations schools reopened. During lunch break standing on the pavement, Babu expected Brother Basheer to come. When he went village fair to buy school books, pens, pencils, etc., he always searched for Brother Basheer. When he was seriously engaged in school happenings memories started vanishing, but not fully forgotten.

On the other side, Brother Basheer always remembered Babu. He always talked about him with his wife. There was not a single day that passed without the reference of Babu the boy.

●

One day when classes were on, Babu heard the voice: 'Peanut Candy.' It is Brother Basheer's voice, Babu was convinced. He fabricated a reason with the teacher and ran to the streets. When both saw each other smiles on their faces. While conversing they reached Babu's home. He made his mother prepare Tea for Basheer, both had it. Babu followed Basheer with his village rounds.

Yet again goon's boys have appeared! First Basheer thought of avoiding them moving forward with a docile feeling. Then suddenly changed his mind. Slow downed his walk. Babu was happy to witness Basheer's courage. Basheer turned and spoke: "What do you think of me? Look at my age. You have to treat and speak with respect." One among the goon's gang dragged Basheer Pajama. Basheer lifted his basket from the head and started yelling at them in an unknown language. You speak in a language we understand, goon boys insisted.

"You do not have any work, other than harassing on-goers?" Basheer asked. The heated arguments continued. Babu was just a witness. One of the goon boys slapped Basheer's galls. They ransacked Basheer's belongings. One among them took all of them with him to home and locked himself, challenging him to take them back if Basheer had guts. Slowly other boys disappeared. Babu comforted Brother Basheer. Somebody gave him a glass of water.

With a cool mind, he stood and walked to the boy's house who had taken his belongings. He tendered an apology and begged to give back his belongings. But the boy never opened the door. Meanwhile, Babu went home and convinced his father, brought him to the scene. When Babu's father looked at the fate of Basheer, felt empathetic. With anger, he knocked on the door and called the boy with a furious voice. The goon boy carried the Bambu basket and set aside it on the bench.

●

Brother Basheer was still crying with the shock. Quietly he carried the basket and started walking. Babu, with the fear of his father, without speaking witnessed Basheer's walk. That was the last day Babu saw Basheer. Twenty-five years have passed. Whenever he hears a vendor's voice, he remembers Brother Basheer and silently cries. When he recalls Basheer's face, his shrill voice is heard saying:

`Peanut Candy'.

■

ASG: Shashikumar, who has won second prize in the competition, is a younger generation writer who has recently published a short story collection, `Byate Mara'. ASG is actively involved in the Kannada film industry. ASG belongs to the Hassan district

3

Golgumbaz Express 16536

Bhagyajyothi Gudageri
Translated by **Rishikesh Bahadur Desai**

The Solapur-Mysore Golgumbaz express train that carries commuters to Bengaluru is all set `to arrive at the platform in a few minutes.

And here I am, feeling extremely tensed with a splitting headache. Why? I cannot escape the thought that he controls my mind, from where ever he is. I feel so angry that I kick myself. The headache continues. I decide to get out of this circle of worry and discomfort, by changing focus.

I move towards the reservation counter to fill out a form and get out of this thought --out. I come to the counter only to find that I have no pen. "Here, Akka, please take this," says a young boy, holding out a pen. He must be just 10 or 12. He lent it to me, though I never asked for it.

I fill out the form, buy the ticket and wait for the train that does not seem to arrive soon. That seems unusually late today, at least by half an hour. I sit quietly, on a wooden bench on the platform in the Bijapur railway station. The platform is crowded. People seem to be engaged in trivialities. Most seem busy on the phone. While some whisper, others are shouting at the top of their voice.

A collage of clouds spreads slowly across the sky.

The train finally arrives, chuffing in with an ear-cracking noise. I can see it slither in, moving across a signal at the far end of the station. Commuters ascend and alight quickly. I climb on, choose a window seat and rest my head on the railing. As I close my eyes, I am lost in thought, chewing on my suppressed grief. A hot wind blows dust across my face. Soon, the overflowing train begins to chuck along. The colours of the evening are slowly painting the sky red.

●

That day, I was in Bengaluru to present a paper on film writing at the Bharatiya Vidya Bhavan. My eyes caught a handsome young man, going around clicking photographs of everyone present, as if to preserve their images for eternity. Average build, curly hair, a beard that hid his chin, and a pleasant smile.

Wearing a black T-shirt and jeans, he keeps running up and down and aisle.

"If you need a photo, this is my number," he went around distributing cards. "Please select your best pics. It is my job to see that it reaches you. I request you to pay me through Google Pay or Phone Pay," he told me before vanishing into the crowd.

That was Arun. We next met at the Krishna Bhavan in Malleshwaram, four days later. I had booked my ticket to Hubballi on a private bus from Anand Rao Circle. But my BFF Ashwini forced me to stay back. " Ashi, I told Mom and Dad that I would be back in two days. It is four days already. They would be worried. Let me go now. I will come later, surely," I convinced her.

"Okay! Now that you are here, let us go shopping in Manthri Mall, eat out and go home," she pulled me along. It was when we sat for lunch post-shopping, that we met Arun.

"Don't tell me you don't want your picture," he said.

"Nothing like that, I need some", I replied.

"But you did not write down your number. Nor did you select an image", he said.

"That is alright, why don't you pick a few that you feel are Okayish", I said when our plates arrived.

"Okay. You carry on. Now that I have your number, I will send you a few. What is your name, by the way?"

"Vani"

"Okay. Bye, Ms. Vani", he smiled and left. He moved swiftly, bypassing those sitting at various tables.

It was thus happenstance that we met the second time. It was not long before we were friends.

Even today, I know very little about Arun's background, but his memories seem to enwrap my heart and mind. Arun, somehow, seemed to have learnt all about me.

Somehow, he seems to charm everyone with his lively chat.

On my birthday, he gifted me a photo frame with a few of my images. That was on my birthday, with a greeting card carrying a message: "Love you Vani".

My feelings were mixed- joy and fear and the ultimate caution that I should not fall for his charms. It seemed that I was attracted to him, gradually. But never did I acknowledge it.

But the pull was too strong to resist. He began to grow on me. My faith in him was getting stronger. But at times, his intimacy felt scary. And one day he broached it. "Let us get married, after convincing all at home", he said. I was tempted to say yes.

Even my images from the photo frame seemed to look at me differently as if to tell me that I had changed in the last few days since I met him.

Meanwhile, my applications to a few colleges in Hubballi Dharwad got favourable responses. A college asked me to join just after I returned from Bengaluru. My parents- Appa and Avva, were very happy. My younger brother Vinay who was in diploma college pleaded: " I would like some pocket money. But please don't tell anyone at home". Avva asked me to go and pray at the Gali Durgamma temple. Break two coconuts there,".

It was Appa's turn to offer wise counsel: " Work hard. See that no one points a finger at you".

What else could he say? He would only talk about adjustment, self-control and being virtuous.

Appa was a meek guy who served as a primary school teacher. He had carried the extended family on his weak shoulders amid debilitating poverty. Decades of drudgery had eroded him from the inside.

However, he never let others know. His peaceful countenance betrayed the deep layers of pain and suffering. Amid such a plight, my job could provide the family some succour. The initial salary I was offered was nothing but peanuts. If I were to work and take some money home regularly, it would help meet our minor expenses, if nothing else. I had often heard Appa confess before Avva in despair: "I could not do much for the children, you see. I feel guilty and helpless". These words were stuck in my mind like an ear bug, for years.

●

I am lost in thought. Pestering issues in my life and my family seem to place a mountain of questions before me. Just as the past was unfolding in front of my eyes, I was jolted back to reality. Someone was pulling my hand.

"Akka, my pen", said the boy who had lent me his. "Sorry, paa. I forgot it in a hurry,"

I said. I quickly unzip my vanity bag, pick up the pen and clip it into his shirt pocket. I want to ask him what was his name. But he is lost in his world. He tears open a packet of chips, devours them in one go and drinks water. I look around and realise that he is unaccompanied. But I don't think much about it. Some more people climb on at Bagewadi. And the boy continues to eat something else.

Just then, I was hit by Arun's betrayal which smashed my resolve of a new life. Tears rush to my eyes and I get up to wash my face. In the wash basin, water is dripping like a thin thread from the faucet. Some loud women sit around in the next bogie. While I can hear their laughter, their talk is all incoherent chatter. The toilet has a very foul smell. The train is reaching the next station, Almatti. Some sit at the door, with their legs stretched out, just to catch a glimpse of the mighty river Krishna.

An old woman with a colourful saree and a bright red bindi catches my eye. She seems attractive for her age. She opens her bosom slightly to pull out a purse and looks for spare change, probably to throw coins in the river. Two middle-aged men accompany her. They must be her children. Marathi-speaking family, I suppose from their conversation. One of them is shouting at the top of his voice. "Let us leave tomorrow immediately after the `Kaka Pinda' rituals. Don't gather a crowd of your relatives and acquaintances. We are fed up with them," he yells. In response, the old woman only mutters something under her breath. "We are tired of telling you repeatedly. But you don't seem to listen. You did not understand anything, even after our home was ruined", he goes on and on.

Now, the whole bogie can hear him shriek.

"All your old kin are bound to destroy our family, but you don't realise that. You cling on to them," screams another, with a scowl. Both are berating the woman, but she seems unconcerned. Her eyes are searching for something outside the compartment. She repeatedly bows to the river and keeps touching her forehead. The dam is visible at a distance. At the Almatti station, not many get down.

A well-built man who came on board sits in the seat in front of me. " Why is your mother standing at the door, ask her to come on over here," I say. "She wants to throw coins in the Krishna. She had taken a vow to do that. I do not know what is achieved with all that. What can I say?" he says.

She is not the only one, though. Countless men and women, bow to the river and throw coins, from the windows and doors of the endless bogies that trudge along. The Marathi woman does the same. I follow suit. I take two coins from my bag and offer them to Mother Krishna. But I ponder. What is this vow? For whom? For what purpose? However, I see that the old woman seems teary-eyed, by doing this.

The Krishna flows silently, undisturbed. The train speeds up. All the travellers are busy with their errands. My eye goes around intently. A young man with ear pads seems drowned in his mobile screen. The young boy who gave me a pen has no one with him. The Marathi woman continues to be silent. She is so pretty that the folds on her face are clearer than the lines on her hand. Her eyes look as if they had sprung out from a portrait. Her neck has a chain with coral beads. Her toothless mouth spews a few words, spraying out saliva. Those with her are quiet, for a change. Their journey which started from Solapur, ends at Bagalkot.

A recorded message on the railway platform repeatedly announces that the train is running behind time for ten minutes. The young boy gets down, eats an idli that has gone cold, drinks juice and climbs down empty rail tracks to urinate. He climbs back again.

I get down too. I am neither hungry nor inclined to eat. But I impulsively buy a pouch of Bindu Jeera. A fellow traveller looks on as I try to pay the vendor unsuccessfully, through UPI.

"Any problem," he asks me. I shake my head. "Don't worry, I will pay. The train will leave now". He pays and we climb on and the train leaves.

"Thank you, ree,"

"Hey, it okay"

"I will give you the change"

"No problem. You, Hubli?"

I shake my head and say " Bengaluru, you?" He clutches his teeth to say he too is travelling. His thick accent betrays his identity. A hard-boiled Malayalee.

"I hail from Hubballi. But I came to Bijapur to attend a meeting. But I have to return to Bengaluru on an urgent call," I say.

"I stay in Bengaluru too. Proper Kerala. I work at Joy Alukkas. I have worked across Karnataka. Ten months in Hubballi. Now, my family is in Bengaluru. I work in different, different branches. Now Airport Road, Kammanahalli branch. Sorry, too much talk. My name is Akhil," he says, extending his hand. I shake his hand and say" Hmm. Vani". He continues to speak. "I came for a friend's marriage. Love cum arranged marriage"......

My mind begins the flight into a haze of turbulence. Arun the charlatan. His sham talk and behaviour come back to hit me like darts. Were they all lies? The promise of marriage on the one hand and conduct that is the exact opposite? Which one is true? All those oaths on God were false? That was not love? Was it just me who was under the delusion? The flower has wilted. The nectar has turned into poison. Was it just sex and lust that he was after, but nothing more? It seems that the walls of infatuation that I had built around myself were collapsing.

●

While my affection for Arun was growing fast and deep, his inner secrets were being exposed one by one.

I found some sleazy pictures in his room and voice records with other women. Chat messages on WhatsApp revealed his double life. He was a bloody creepy pervert! I was only one among the many girls he had gathered around. It seemed that he considered women as chattel to buy and sell. He used photography to lure and seduce them.

In my case, as he gained control over me, his voice got harsher and his acts became violent. His chatter which felt like sweet nothings initially, ended up sounding like air bubbles that went splosh! When I confronted him, came to tears, fell at my feet and begged me to forgive him. But then it was short-lived. It was part of an elaborately staged drama. At once he would be humble, polite and loyal and at other times, he used to mount me like a demon.

Even this routine seemed well rehearsed. I began feeling that I was caught in a trap. I suffered violent assaults and repeated abuse. My suffering had no end.

Well, this is no life. At least not the one that I sought. What is this life if I willingly get sucked into such a cesspool? I lost count of the days and nights I had spent in such an agonising ordeal.

●

Akhil opens his lunch box, saying that the newlyweds would return to Bengaluru in a week. “My friend’s mother packed this for me,” he says with a smile. The Chapatis roll out of the newspaper. First, I refuse his offer to eat. “Arre, don’t worry, you can surely have a bite,” he says. He plates two Chapatis with a lump of the gram flour sabzi and sprouts and hands it to me. His box packs enough for two and more.

The young boy looks around forlorn. He keeps sipping water as if to wet his throat.

“Why don’t you come here, lad,” I call him. Akhil gives him some food too. “What is your name?”, I ask the boy. “Why is no one with you? Are you travelling alone?”. “No. I am not alone. We are on a study tour from our school. The rest are in the other bogie,” he says.

The answer is not innocent enough to be credible. It raises many questions. Why is such a small boy travelling alone? How will go to the big bad city of Bengaluru on his own? I feel concerned, but all that seemed minute compared to my predicament. I ask again:” What is your name?” “Manikantha, Akka,” he says, takes the Chapati roll and returns to his seat. He seems to be disoriented. Hence, he has no sense of hunger or satiety.

I get up, tie my dupatta around my nose, visit the washroom and come back. The girl sitting on the top berth is speaking to her dad on her phone: “Appa, I will be fine. Don’t worry. Please go home safely. I will be safe too. Please tell Grandma and Grandpa that I asked for them. I will call as soon as I reach”. The girl seems confident. By this time, the train had crossed towns like Guledagudda, Badami and Hole Alur. I had not noticed them though. The train is now stationed in Gadag junction.

Akhil says he was feeling sleepy. "Are you not?", he asks before closing his eyes.

●

Unable to control the urge to call Arun, I dial his number. He has blocked it. That is nothing new. He kept blocking my number and then calling me back, and then blocking me again. It was all very weird. Why should I go to Bengaluru to chase someone like this? What will I achieve? Is it wise to get down at Hubballi, mid-way? The confusion blurs my eyes.

Akhil has got down to stretch his legs. He climbs up at the signal. He looks fresh after a few minutes of rest. Manikanth is fast asleep. I feel thirsty. Akhil seems to have sensed it. He raises his eyebrows to ask me: "What?". "Water," I say. He gives me a bottle. However, I can not hold the bottle steady due to the jerky movement of the train. A little water spills on my neck and chest. This directs some young eyeballs towards me. One of them keeps staring at my chest. Akhil intervenes. He sits beside me and asks the young man with a stank face:" What happened?". Reality dawns. Akhil asks me if I am alright.

Human nature confounds me. But then, nothing seems to surprise me lately. If the dark sides of men are revealed to me, I neither notice them, nor am I troubled by them. My mind forgets some facets while it savours others, even though they remain strangers.

The train stopped at Hubballi junction, after passing through Annigeri. The clock says it is 11 at night. The recorded messages in the platform continue to be announced in multiple languages: "Your attention, please. Train number 16536 Golgumbaz Express from Solapur to Mysuru has arrived at platform number 4".

The station is full of commuters who have arrived from far-off places. Some of them have gone to sleep, waiting for their trains.

Those awake exchange glances with strangers. Gang men are watching over the tracks. Ticket Examiners, some in dark coats, some in white shirts, meet in groups and span out. I sit with Akhil on an iron bench. The night is humid. The grandpa clock yawns to say it is 11.20. Neon lights on large hoardings scream for advertisements of products and services.

I see that Manikanth took a Rs 500 note to a shop and bought a packet of Mishra Pedha. I wonder how such a small boy can carry such a big note. I have never seen anyone accompanying him, all through the journey. I am convinced that he is lying.

I tell Akhil all about the boy. "Oh! Seems serious. It is a sensitive issue, but I will handle it. You can be wrong, too," he said. The young girl who had come from Bagalkot is on the platform, walking aimlessly while speaking on her phone.

Railway staff are filling water to the train engine. A team of young boys is cleaning the station. Porters who were filling the water tank, stop after it overflowed. Despite the cleaning, I could see giant rats running around on the train. Some train engines are hissing and burping to start. Some other porters are loading fish boxes, big bags, and iron implements on the train. Two other express trains to Bengaluru leave the station. I wash my face with the tap on the platform.

The train is now cleaner than before. I feel a change in my mood. It seemed as if there was some cleaning going on inside me too. The desire to get down at Hubballi is going away. The train is now full of passengers. Ticket examiners get ready to climb on. Golgumbaz Express bids goodbye to Hubballi. We got on:- me and the girl, and Manikantha.

The fresh cold wind blowing across my face reminds me that I am no longer tense. I take a few deep breaths. The stand that I need to take in the future is getting clearer. Four members of a family have occupied seats in my bogie. They are going to Bengaluru for a loved one's treatment. Their tension and insecurity are obvious. No one probes them further.

When I speak to Manikanth again, he gives incoherent answers. "Who are your friends? Where is your teacher? Why has no one come to see you here?" No answers. Finally, Akhil threatened him that he would report him to the police if he did not tell the truth. In response, he begins to shiver. "My uncle is a driver in Bengaluru. He will pick me up," he stammers. When we bombard him with further questions like "What does your father do? Which is your native village?", he opens up, albeit fearfully. "My father is a driver with the State-run bus service. We live in Indi," he says.

By then, the ticket examiner and some other travellers have gathered around us. Someone calls the KSRTC depot in Bijapur. They trace Manikantha's father Rachappa Patil, and succeed in contacting him. Mr Patil is relieved to find that the boy who had run away from home, has been traced. I am hailed as the girl who rescued the boy who strayed. I take the phone and explain everything to the father. "How is he, Amma? He has run away just because we tried to discipline him for skipping school,", he says. He thanked us profusely, saying they were feeling let down. The ticket examiner also speaks to Rachappa Patil. The officers take Manikantha away. The boy's feelings, however, are mixed. His eyes seem to shine once and throw a child-like glance at another time.

Akhil asks me to remain calm. "I will go and find out what happens next". "Manikanth'a uncle will come to Yashwanthpur to pick him up," he tells me later.

As if he had read my mind, Akhil came up with a philosophical quote. "Vani Avare, Life is small. But it is beautiful. We have to go along living it without hassles," he says before going back to sleep.

When he closes his eyes, I feel like he is laughing silently and notice his rounded cheeks. I fall asleep too. When I open my eyes, the skyline is filled with huge buildings. Though the train is nearing Bengaluru, it is not Yashwanthpur yet. It has stopped, probably to give way to a goods train at a signal crossing. I am thirsting for coffee. I look at the rising morning and a glowing Akhil. The train journey seems to have greatly changed my mood. My woes have disappeared from the experience of meeting people en route and seeing their problems. The morning has washed off my worries. Akhil is waiting with a cup of coffee in his hand. The scattered crowd, formed by commuters that had got down on the platform, climbs back up.

When the train reaches Bengaluru, the crowd turns to a mob trying to alight quickly. My mind has buried the memories of Arun in an unknown corner. All my delusions seem to have washed off, too. I am feeling relieved and my mind is unburdened. All the confusions in life have been resolved and everything is crystal clear. There is a smile on my face. And a new energy in my limbs. Manikantha has broken into a run as he tries to keep up with the ticket examiner. Behind him is Akhil.

Some passengers get ready to get off at the next station.

Ultimately, all of us have to get down at some station, right? If the current station is not ours, we should keep travelling further and get off at the next, right?

With calmness, I pick up my bag. A new life awaits when I catch the next train or bus.

■

Bhagyajyothi Gudageri, a poet, has published two collections of poems. Her recent anthology of poems, `Bidira Binnaha', has attained critical appreciation. She is also a voice artist for a radio station. Her story was selected for the third prize by the jury. Bhagyajyothi is a native of Dharwad district.

Rishikesh Bahadur Desai is a correspondent for The Hindu, an English newspaper. He writes extensively on social and cultural issues of Karnataka state. His active involvement with both Kannada and English languages has contributed significantly to the development of both languages. Additionally, Desai has translated Praveen Kumar Honnakudari's short story, "Keelya," for this anthology.

4

A Distressed Soul

Deepa Hiregutti

Translated by **S. Jayasrinivasa Rao**

Mr Raghurama Shetty, the landlord, in all these years, had never once ventured near their 'room.' Whenever Mr Shetty saw him, he would only ask, "*Going to your workplace?*" or "*Returning from work?*" and go his way. Now that Mr. Shetty had climbed up three floors and come to his 'room' and scanned the room skeptically, made Sandesh strangely uneasy.

Always clad in a white *panche* and a crisp white shirt, Mr Shetty would always be seen stroking his striking bushy white moustache with his right hand. He wielded his cane-handle umbrella like a walking stick, and his walk was accompanied by that unmistakable *charr ... parr ...* sound his Kolhapuri sandals made. Mr Raghurama Shetty, all of seventy, looked impressive and made heads turn wherever he went. His two sons were in foreign lands, and so Mr Shetty handled all business matters and he also had a couple of houses rented out. One such building was this apartment with three houses, which was not an 'apartment' per se. On the terrace of this apartment was a one-room house built with concrete sheets. Along with his friends, Sandesh was one of the tenants who lived in this room. The reason why Sandesh was worried about Mr. Shetty's unexpected arrival was not that he had unpaid rent or that he had done something unsavory.

He had wanted to tell Mr. Shetty about an unusual dilemma he was stuck in, but couldn't bring himself up to say it. Sandesh was a shy man by nature and this unexpected visit by Mr Shetty had made him feel all the more guilty like the man who did not steal the pumpkin but still felt about his shoulder whenever someone shouted 'pumpkin.'

Sandesh was born into a lower-middle-class family in a village in the Malenadu part of Karnataka. By the time he somehow managed to pass his pre-university course in second class, he had developed an allergy to books. He could never comprehend English and Economics even if he were to do endless somersaults. "*'Waste bodies' who can't even score 'pass' marks*," the lecturer would taunt them. Swallowing such insults, he somehow passed his pre-university course. He struggled again for three years during his undergraduate course. Even after all the 'labor work,' he only managed a 'just pass' here too. As a result, he couldn't find a proper job. Around this time e-commerce had started becoming popular in smaller towns too. Consequently, the 'delivery executive' jobs that were available only in bigger cities, were now available everywhere. This came as a silver lining around the edges of disappointing dark clouds of unemployment for lots of young men like Sandesh. He took up this job as it offered him a source of livelihood. For a salary of Rs.13,000, he had to travel up to the taluk town and return home every day. His home was in a village located 50 kilometers away, which could only be approached through an untarred road. He managed to find two more boys with whom he could share a small house and its rent, found a house in the taluk town, and moved in there. This small house was near the office-cum-warehouse of his company and located in the heart of the town. The house had a long hall, a small kitchen, and a bathroom. The long hall was the bedroom, and it was the dining room too. And for this small house, he paid Rs.4,500 as rent. Sandesh was an introvert and would have liked to live alone, but the idea of the rent amount divided by three was a bigger incentive; and so, he made the extra effort to find two more boys to share this house and rent.

Mr Shetty had told them categorically that only the three of them could live in the house and relatives and other guests could not come and stay there for days on end. Of the other two house-mates, Karthik worked in a fruit shop and Praveen worked in a bakery. Though it was decided initially that the rent would be shared equally among the three, Sandesh decided to bear the lion's share as sharing the rent equally would have placed a heavier burden on the other two who earned only around seven or eight thousand rupees per month. And so, he told them to give only one thousand rupees each. This gesture came as a surprise to the other two who realised that this serious-looking man was soft-hearted. They had thanked him profusely with gratitude-filled eyes. They cooked and ate together and after spending on groceries, vegetables, and petrol, they were able to send some money home to their parents. By the time the month came to a close, they would wait eagerly for their salaries, like farmers in May looking forward to the monsoon.

Troubles don't come alone, they come in waves, one after the other, he had read or heard somewhere, and this held for Sandesh in his life. All of a sudden, his mother's kidneys stopped functioning. The dialysis machine at the Taluk government hospital had broken down years ago. So, he had to take her to the district government hospital, for which they had to travel 70 kilometers by bus, one way. He would need at least three thousand rupees for each trip. After his father's passing away, he and his elder brother were the only earning members in the family. Despite working hard, their salaries remained the same and they would be at their wit's end. They had to take care of so many things – to give a proper education to their younger sister, look after household expenses, and meet the medical expenses of their mother – and they had to allocate their limited salaries to meet these expenses. Both of them had to invariably apply for leave at least twice a week, which amounted to around eight to nine days every month. Each took four days off from work only to take their mother to the hospital. Both brothers had no option but to swallow their fatigue and go on working without a day's rest. While they did not mind the hard work, the thought of cringing and begging before their bosses every time they wanted a day off made them feel sick of their miserable lives.

As the cost of his mother's treatment and household expenses began to mount, Sandesh began to feel that earning every single rupee was a struggle. And in the middle of all this chaos, his sister-in-law's pregnancy was confirmed. On one of the ensuing days, his elder brother called him aside and said with tears in his eyes, "*You know that my wife works in the cloth store. She can't go to work now. I can contribute financially for only one more month now. You'll have to somehow manage now.*" "*Let's see what happens, you don't worry Anna,*" said Sandesh, as he gently patted his brother's back and consoled him.

Sandesh had to make a delivery at a house some distance away and while returning along the lonely wooded path, he stopped his bike and cried his heart out. Every time he would pass the Ganapati Temple near his office, he would make a gesture of prayer touching his lips and chest with his thumb and forefinger of his right hand. "*Oh God, my shoulders are tired carrying all this weight, how much more weight are you going to pile up?*" he would beseech with a sigh.

The small-mindedness of some of the people he encountered while delivering items made him sick. A high-ranking officer had once purchased a product through cash-on-delivery that cost Rs.980, and he gave Sandesh Rs.1,000 when he delivered it. Sandesh had two ten-rupee notes with him and gave these notes back as change. The officer returned one ten-rupee note as it was slightly torn and asked Sandesh to give him a clean note. Sandesh did not have any other ten-rupee note with him. The officer too did not have any change. But this officer did not allow Sandesh to leave till he gave him a clean note. Sandesh went around the local shops looking for a better-looking note till he got one! But not everyone behaved this way. Some customers asked him to keep the change, some others would give him a small tip of ten or twenty rupees. Despite all these, his earnings were like a small mattress that could neither support his head nor reach his feet.

Sandesh was unable to sleep well with his legs touching the floor, and neither was he in a position to buy a new mattress. While in this clueless state, one of his regular customers, a lady, called him on his phone one day. "*Sandesh, some of my relatives will be paying a visit shortly. They informed me only a few minutes ago. My husband is not in town and I don't have the time to cook a full-course meal for them. I'll give you a list of dishes that I want, could you get them for me from this restaurant, please?*" she requested. This lady would always give him a small tip of ten or twenty rupees whenever he made a delivery to their house. And so, he agreed and went to the restaurant she had mentioned, bought the dishes, and delivered them to her house. She thanked him profusely and happily gave him a large hundred-rupee tip. After this episode, on other occasions too, she had requested him to deliver food to their house, and a couple of times, to her other lady-friends homes too. He sensed a demand for this kind of service and wondered why he shouldn't start a delivery service himself.

So, what began as a food delivery service under the name, 'Sandesh Home Delivery Service,' now covered the entire taluk. This tiny one-man business delivered anything and everything to anybody with just a phone call. And he delivered everything without exception – groceries, medicines, vegetables, breakfast, lunch, eatables, and so on. He charged only Rs.30 for each delivery. People felt it was cheaper to pay Rs.30 to Sandesh and get the items delivered than go to the market, spend time there, spending on fuel, or pay autorickshaw hire charges. Apart from these, the other advantage was that Sandesh had all the information at his fingertips – names of all the dishes available at all the hotels, which dishes tasted good, which hotels made the best food, their cost, etc. And so, a lot of people began to rely on Sandesh as it was advantageous on all counts.

For people living on the outskirts of the town, senior citizens, and for those living alone, Sandesh's delivery service was a boon. Now, whenever guests dropped in without notice, it was not a problem to procure milk snacks or fruit. This venture, which started small, slowly grew into an extremely busy venture only through word-of-mouth publicity. Orders would keep coming in throughout the day, and late into the night. And because of this home delivery business, Sandesh's earnings saw an increase. But since his elder brother had stopped giving his share of money towards household expenses, this extra money that Sandesh earned went to cover that deficit. When a storm throws you in the middle of a raging sea, even a rickety boat offers hope of safety, thought Sandesh and tried to console himself.

But there was always this anxiety. Yes, it was tough for his brother too. Yet, he was unable to decide if it was right on his part to agree to shoulder the entire responsibility of the household. A couple of days earlier, when his younger sister wanted something and asked his elder brother, he instead told her to ask Sandesh for it. His elder brother was supposed to take Amma for her dialysis this weekend. "*You can ask others to get your work done, Sandesh, but I have no more leaves left*," he had moaned. Just because he had agreed to shoulder the burden of household expenses out of family obligations, his brother through his clever arguments was now trying to hoist more responsibilities on Sandesh. Though Sandesh understood his brother's ploy to divest himself of responsibilities, he decided to keep quiet. But what pained Sandesh most was his brother's thinking that Sandesh was a total fool. In this selfish world where you become your advocate and sit in judgment over others, Sandesh always advocated the cause of others and sat in judgment over his actions, and he knew that this was the cause of all his pain and misery. But his mind also kept telling him that he was making the same mistake again and again. Then he promises himself that this time probably would be the last time and hereafter, he would fight his case! This promise never changes, and nothing ever changes. He requested another delivery boy, a friend, to handle his orders and got on the bus to take his mother for her dialysis.

On some days when he would return home and relax after a full day's delivery routine, Sandesh would feel that he had given too much freedom to his dreams. Many a time he would wonder if he would have been more at peace if he had allowed his dreams to travel only as far as he was able to go. He would correct himself immediately and say, "*No, surely not. It is only because I allowed my dreams to run ahead while I followed them that I was able to start this small business! That too, something which nobody had even thought about in the entire taluk.*" Once, when he was in the second year of his pre-university course, the Economics professor had asked in class – "*What would you like to become in the future?*" "*Ma'am, I want to become an entrepreneur,*" said one of the class toppers. The professor was impressed and asked the entire class to cheer and applaud the boy. Sandesh, who hadn't even known what the word meant, was clueless and sullen. But now, he had become an 'entrepreneur' much before that class topper, and this, Sandesh felt, was because life is a large open field of immense possibilities and he was now convinced that any new idea that benefits people would always be welcome. What if he had been scared of failure and had told his dreams to be careful before taking the next step? He would be walking around carrying the constantly stabbing nail of dissatisfaction in his heart because, without his consent, his heart would not have had the courage to follow its dreams this far.

The next moment, he remembered Tripti. She worked as a supervisor in his earlier workplace. When he saw her on his first day of work, he felt a quiver pass through him and believed that he now had a reason not to miss even a single day's work. An attractive girl with large black eyes, he happily experienced the thrill of dreaming that if this girl would only smile at him, he would fall in love with her. Sometimes, he felt that he could happily forget the burning reality of his life if only he could lay down for a while in the shade of the moonlight radiating from her eyes. But it did take not long for him to realize that he would be relaxing under the shade of a cobra's hood.

For her, delivery boys were beneath contempt. Nobody had any objections to her dreams of a charming prince riding on horseback crossing the seven seas and coming to rescue her from this world of troubles. But her big mistake was to believe that this office was her palace and those poor boys working there for paltry four-figure salaries were her slaves and so, of no consequence. She made it a habit to insult these boys based on flimsy complaints by customers. When she insulted him and sneered at him, he would notice her enthusiasm, that feeling of victory in her eyes as if she had discovered something precious ... in the way she turned up her pert nose, and curled those lovely lips! "*Abba, I wouldn't have believed that beauty could arouse fear and loathing at the same time until I experienced it personally.*" But it was still a mystery to Sandesh as to why she hated him so much. In a way, it was good. Like a drowning man gasping for breath and somehow finding a way to live, Sandesh was proud of himself that he forged a new path and managed to emerge out of that situation and survive.

As he started believing that everything was on track and running smoothly, Mr. Shetty's coming to their house made Sandesh tremble with guilt even as he was riding his bike. On that day, as he was thinking and riding, he hadn't noticed the speed-breaker. He hit the speed-breaker at full speed and his bike flew high up in the air. But he escaped by a hair's breadth, and fortunately, did not sustain any major injuries. It was not that the issue that he was thinking about so fervidly was something very serious, but it was also not something that could be brushed aside as frivolous!

So, this is what had happened. Officially, only three boys were staying in that house, but at night two more boys would come in and sleep, wake up early in the morning, brush, bathe, and leave. If the story of those three boys was gloomy, the story of these two boys was miserable. One of them was Rakshit and the other was Sanchit. Both worked in petrol stations for awfully meagre salaries. They were not strong enough for physical labor, nor were they used to that sort of work. Their financial situation was so bad that they did not have any money with them either at the beginning of the month or at its end. "*Please, somehow adjust and help us for some time, Sandesh Anna, we will come in at midnight and leave at five in the morning,*" they had beseeched Sandesh and his heart melted in the face of their pitiable condition. *It's all right, they will come in late at night, wake up early the next day, bathe, and leave. How will Mr Shetty know? Even if he gets to know I will tell him that an old friend of mine had dropped in to see me after a long time*, he told himself and kept quiet about it.

If there are so many stories of misery in this small taluk, what would Bangalore be like with its teeming population, how many more sufferings, Sandesh would sometimes ponder? Forget Bangalore, even here, each person's story is of a different kind. His story and the stories of the four people who shared this house, each story is different. There was Karthik, who had hoped to make a living driving an autorickshaw and had purchased one on loan. The autorickshaw was badly damaged in an accident and his dreams were put on hold. Now, he didn't have the money to pay for the extensive repairs; and on top of that, he had to take up a job to pay the EMIs for the autorickshaw. Then there was Praveen, who was saving money to get the old family house in the village repaired. Rakshit, who had run away from home to escape his parents' alcoholism, now cries to sleep every night out of grief of abandonment. And Sanchit struggles to pay EMIs for the smartphone he bought for his sister. She was studying in the first year of her undergraduate course and her college had told her, categorically, not to attend classes without a smartphone. If their stories of want are of this kind, then on the other side there are those with means who buy loads of stuff online! When Sandesh worked as a delivery boy, he would deliver goods worth thousands and lakhs of rupees, and sometimes he would visit the same house two or three times a day to deliver goods. And whenever he saw that the value of a single order was sometimes ten times that of his monthly salary, he would gulp in surprise. There was, perhaps, not a single day where he didn't think about why life had been so unkind to people like him.

The boys who came in at midnight would arrive with defeated faces, guzzle water copiously, and go to bed. When he saw this being repeated almost every day, Sandesh instinctively knew that they had not eaten anything. One day, as they were ready to go to bed, Sandesh said, "*Hei, look, however carefully I measure and cook rice, I always manage to make more than required. My mother has sent chicken curry, why don't you eat and then go to bed.*" They hesitated, and so he brought out the plates and served them. When they finished eating their eyes were filled with an inexplicable emotion. After this episode, Sandesh would often keep aside two plates with rice and sambar for them and go to sleep. Guessing that they would feel embarrassed if he did this every day, he skipped some days in between. But since he did not want to disappoint the boys who returned late at night expecting a meal, he would bring some bananas or egg puffs for them.

On holidays sometimes they would buy biriyani parcels and sit together and eat and chat in the open terrace outside their room. "*Shall I call Sandesh Home Delivery Service and ask him to deliver five biriyanis?*" someone would say and another would drawl dramatically, "*Why should we pay him thirty rupees, I'll go and get them.*" Then they would all look at Sandesh with mischief in their eyes. If they spied a smile on his lips, they would all laugh all the more. Sandesh had always been a loner and had few friends. Sometimes it would seem like he spread his lonesomeness to those around him. He always behaved as if he had lost something and he was searching for that something not knowing what it was. When he met Tripti the first time, he felt a warm and pleasant wave caress his heart. But the bitter experience with her made him wary like a cat that had once put its mouth in a pot of hot milk. After this, he was even scared to dream. On one of the rare occasions when he would go out to watch a movie, he would feel that only people like him became heroes of tragic love stories where love ended before it even began. Like those children who grew up in dire difficulties and who seemed to age prematurely, Sandesh always carried an air of seriousness with him. Even though the circumstances of the other boys too were more or less the same, they would indulge in some fun now and then. Sometimes they would laugh at their own predicaments, saying that they are so unlucky that when they felt suffocated in their room and came out to look at the sky, even the stars run away. Apart from these moments of levity, these boys, three of them between 24 and 27 years of age and two of them below 20, would always look grave, like soldiers getting ready for the next day's battle.

And, on that day Sandesh was sitting outside his room thinking furiously, why had Mr Shetty come up to their room? Did one of us tell him about our secret arrangement? A thought flashed through his mind. "*In this sparrow's nest of a small room, how fair is it for five of us to sleep here, when only three of us can stay?*" one of his roommates, Praveen had raised the issue. "*It's all right, Praveen, let it be,*" Sandesh tried to pacify him. But Praveen had persisted. "*They could at least give Rs.500 each, no? The money could come in handy for daily expenses,*" he grumbled. Sandesh got a bit worked-up at this comment. "*Now, look Praveen, if we are talking about sharing expenses equally, then you should be giving Rs.1,500. But initially, when I said you may give only Rs.1,000, you were so happy, weren't you? These are young boys, forget it.*" Sandesh realized that he had raised his voice without meaning to and that Praveen might have felt offended thinking that he had reprimanded him. He wondered if he had taken a risk by saying thus to Praveen because there was no question of leaving this room at any cost. Though the taluk was small in size, and the houses waiting for tenants were also small, the rent amount everywhere was big. And it was impossible to get a house for rent so close to the town center. He was worried that Mr Shetty might come to know of their arrangement and ask them to leave. Then he consoled himself by saying that staying in this house was important to Praveen too.

When he returned home at 10 o'clock after making a late-night delivery, he saw Mr Shetty taking a walk near the wall of his house, waiting for Sandesh. When he saw Mr Shetty, his heart came to his mouth. Fortunately, there was nobody else around. He tried to control his pounding heart as he opened the gate and greeted, "*Namaskara, Mr Shetty, did you have your dinner?*" "*No, I haven't eaten yet. I wanted to tell you something and since it is a full moon tonight, I thought I'd take a walk while I waited for you,*" Mr. Shetty said. Oh God, I should have told him about this earlier, and now, that time has passed, Sandesh rued. He prayed fervently for time to stop at this very moment so that Mr Shetty need not say anything at all.

Mr Shetty started speaking, "*See, Sandesh, I wanted to speak to you about this. It's nothing. Summer is approaching and you people are finding it difficult to sleep at night under the asbestos sheet roof, no? I had thought of replacing the sheets with roof tiles last year itself, but I had some financial issues. This time, I will raise the wall a bit higher and replace the sheets with roof tiles. I will also get two ceiling fans installed. You people will have to find some alternative accommodation for the next four or five days till the renovation work is completed. You needn't take your things; I'll have them safely covered with tarpaulin sheets. Is this fine with you?*" Sandesh was stunned and speechless at this unexpected, but welcome turn the topic had taken. Mr Shetty sensed something else behind Sandesh's silence and said, "*If you are worried that I will increase the rent immediately, I won't. We'll think about it next year, don't worry. I'll leave now,*" he said, gave Sandesh a pat on his back, and left. The anxiety that was weighing him down for more than a week suddenly lifted and he felt a lot lighter. He sat down on the steps and rested his head against the wall. He kept staring at the golden colored full-moon. He could feel the honeyed moonbeams and the cool breeze caressing him. Sandesh's eyes brimmed over and he started sobbing silently.

■

Deepa Hiregutti is a lecturer by profession and also a prolific writer. `Parimalavillada Hoogala Madhye' is her first collection of poems. `Solemba Geluvu' is a nonfiction book published by Deepa. She is a native of Uttara Kannada district.

S. Jayasrinivasa Rao, who has translated Deepa's story, is a well-known translator and professor of language and literature. His translations of various poets from different parts of the world into Kannada are widely read on social media.

5

Ebb and Tide

Praveen Kumar G

Translated by **Akarsha Kamala Ramesh**

'You seem to have got your libido back after 8 years of marriage,' quipped Anu. The evening breeze that carried Anu's sarcasm did not caress the partner. An abstract burden heavy in Manohar's chest turned a deaf ear. He had been raking in a lot of money from his recent high-ranking job in a firm called Instrutech (He had made the switch about 3 months ago). Seemingly inspired by the quote 'Do not save money. Instead, invest in life and its experiences.' 'Do not leave behind assets for your kids. Instead, turn your kids into your best asset.' 'Yes, the quotes made sense, but to turn kids into assets, kids need to exist in the first place, right? So, let us experience life instead.' Manohar and Anu's humorous take on these quotes was not aimed at deflecting the seriousness of their decision to not have kids soon. They had always been opposed to the societal idea that 'Kids are not a burden. They bloom naturally.' On the contrary, they thought 'Kids are God's blessings. You ought to give them all the attention they seek. They should not be devoid of anything. You should bestow upon them the luxuries and necessities of the world. Only when we possess the ability to take care of them and pamper them that is when we shall have kids.' When Anu said this on the eve of their first marriage anniversary Manohar agreed and nodded his head. It had been 8 years since their marriage, and they had adhered to this decision of theirs.

But the subject under consideration was not that of having kids. It was their honeymoon trip. He had been weighed down by the burden of life; an educational loan to complete his engineering, his twin sister's marriage, and a new home in his hometown Raichur; all his responsibilities as an elder son had ended and money was finally beginning to make its way to Manu's pockets. His parents had rented out their house and had settled in the elder sister's house in America. They stuck to their schedule of 'skyping' every fifteen days. 'Not everyone has a yearning for their hometown!'

His younger sister's story was quite intriguing. The fact that her husband was now a popular Instagram influencer, and a content creator made her proud. Her husband had graduated from the same college as Manu. Umesh had been recruited by a prestigious MNC in an on-campus recruitment. After working for two years Umesh had called it quits. I fail to understand if people are dumb or if the videos have a real sense of entertainment. As far as Manu was concerned, he had never found them to be hilarious or something close enough to being funny. Manu was infuriated with Umesh for coercing Anu to act in his videos and essentially cloning his lunatic behavior. Her reels have garnered her about 400,000 followers on Instagram. She loved persuading Manu to collaborate with her occasionally and turned ecstatic when her videos became viral. Manu's happiness lay in her happiness too. However, he was brooding over the fact that he had to resign from his current job.

2

Today was Monday. A new week's first tomorrow. A day that would bring with it a new ray of hope. He anticipated the release of the offer letter from his dream company Medi World. While walking over to his cabin and delegating the tasks for the current week, Sandhya smiled and said, 'Anu's new reel is viral. Ask her to ward off the evil eye. By the way, you too.' Fatigue adorned Manu as he patiently waited for that email. 'Women can do anything they want, but the husband is the one who always needs to slog his ass off.' Sandhya didn't pay heed to what he uttered and simply walked away because she too was an ardent reel fan. Manu had been working in Light Med company ever since he graduated from his engineering university and the recent job (about three months ago) that he had secured at Instrutech company had everything going for him. The fact that he was resigning from his current job was the source of Sandhya's agony.

Instrutech had conveyed to Manu on Friday that they would put together a contractual document highlighting all the details including salary, benefits, and joining date, and mail it on Monday after getting the MD's official authorization. It was noon and when he grew impatient after not hearing back from them, he walked into the cafeteria and called them. 'We are sorry Manohar; your profile is unfortunately not approved.' The mellifluous voice of the woman on the other end of the line had shattered all his dreams.

Manu was angry and irked. He tried to leverage his network to find out the person who had secured the position. He had enough information that only ten people were in consideration, and it was mostly the people in his network. A few phone calls brought to light the identity of the person. It was Ashika, who worked as his junior in the Light Med company for two years. Bitch! Those were the words that first came to him. 'That asshole MD would have told her 'If you sleep with me you can sit in my chair' and being the bitch, she would have stripped naked without any hesitation. Such a hierarchical slut'. Realizing that the source of his insomnia was the cups of black coffee, he stopped drinking them after noon. It was now beyond 5 pm. While his disquieted self sat in the cafeteria he drank two black coffees violating the self-imposed dietary rules. It was at this time that a message popped up on his WhatsApp 'Goa next week?' He realized that it was the last week of the third month since he joined this company, and it made him despondent. He was obligated to respond to the message. The fear of the unknown lingered in the air. When the very environment he was in started fading slowly complemented by an obscure visual image, Sandhya (he had scolded her in the morning) joined him for a cup of coffee.

Manu said, 'Sorry Sandhya'. She didn't realize why. She had just finished half of her coffee when she stopped and replied, 'It should be me who should be saying sorry Manu. I kept pestering my husband to create reels. For the first time, I understood the vex that reels can cause to men after analyzing your reaction. I won't trouble him henceforth. Thank you for this life-changing lesson'. 'Whatever happens in life women only comprehend what they want to and how they want to' Manu smirked. Thanks again he said. She got up and said, 'See you' and went away. When she got out of the cab this morning, Manu could have texted her Sorry. But Manu hated texting. He always believed in face-to-face conversations and that a genuine sorry uttered by looking into the other person's eyes is the only way to get rid of the guilt. The apology had brought relief and he replied with a YES to the 'Goa next week?' text message he had received. He re-lived this 'YES' moment by again sipping a cup of black coffee.

3

When there were new board members appointed to the Light Med company four months ago, Manu's life dramatically changed. The ethics and professionalism that had traveled with him for 13-14 years in the same company were given two hoots by the new board members. They had promoted the employees with even lesser experience and given them powerful designations which led to his frustration reaching its peak. They pretentiously branded him the best performer of the year and gave him a good increment. That didn't excite him. Money can be the sole driving agent for a while. After that, life teaches you that it's power that would bring respect and enliven your work. That instigated him to resign from Light Med and pursue other opportunities. He had not been successful so far.

The afternoon that saw him cursing his company and the domain he was working in was complemented by a packed lunch from

Anu that included chapati, beans, curd, and sprouted green gram. The morose setting also brought in WhatsApp messages of his counterparts boasting about the job switch that they made to prestigious firms. He stood in front of the lake at the Orion Mall and saw an eagle sit atop one of those decorative trees. 'I wanted to fly like an eagle and soar above all my friends', he thought to himself while his phone rang displaying an unknown number.

'Hello, Am I speaking to Mister Manohar?' 'Yes, it's me'. 'I am Neha from the HR team of Instrutech. If you are interested, we have an opening for the position of South Manager of India. We would like to set up a meeting with our South Executive Director,' she said. It was hard for him to digest. Because Instrutech was one of the top 10 companies in India designing and manufacturing medical equipment. He had only aspired for a regional position in Karnataka and now he was being considered for a position that handled the whole of South India. His excitement grew beyond the boundaries that the new job had to offer. 'Yes', he replied to which Neha said, 'I will call you back'.

Manu immediately called Anu. Anu was ecstatic about the fact because it validated her belief in the horoscope reader and his predictions, which always seemed to turn out to be true. He had predicted about a week ago that Anu and Manu would be at the crossroads of the biggest decision of their lives. This news excited Anu and she heaped praises on the horoscope reader. 'In my dream last night, I was wearing a glittering diamond necklace,' said Anu. 'Were there no diamond earrings?' asked Manu. 'You know it's always pieced together as a set Manu'. Aha, he said and they both laughed. When Manu reached home the smell of his favourite carrot halwa and dal khichdi reminded him of the Sarvajna triplet 'To have a partner who satisfies your every desire is analogous to heaven'.

About two weeks later, there was a rendezvous arranged with Instrutech's Amit at Taj West End on Race Course Road at 7 pm. Dim lights and faint music set up the ambiance of the restaurant. There were tables and chairs with about 5 people spread across and two waiters. After waiting for about ten minutes and staring at the darkness being engulfed by light, Manu saw Amit walking towards him. He knew Amit. Amit's reputation preceded his name in the organization. Amit must be around 40 years old. Manu had interacted with him at multiple company events and product launches. He had shaken hands with him and had brief discussions. When he learned that Amit was originally from Bangalore, his belief that Bangalore-born engineers always rose to fame grew stronger. The fact that he held a powerful reputed position at such a young age made him look up to Amit. Manu was 35 and for an employee who had envisioned his goals to be at least half of what Amit had achieved, a stroke of luck had laid everything in front of him.

After Manu got up and shook hands with Amit, Amit asked him to sit down. 'We are happy to have you, Manu'. Manu said, 'Pleasure is mine.' 'I know people like you can take our company to greater heights' said Amit to which Manu replied, 'In an organization such as yours everybody tends to automatically bring their best to the table'. They both knew that these were 'tailored for the corporate' statements loaded with pre-programmed emotions. That's probably why Manu refused to address Amit as Sir throughout the conversation. When the waiter came in to get their order, Amit asked him 'What do you have' to which the waiter replied, 'Veg or Non-Veg sir'. 'Pure veg man. One plate of Idli now and Veg Biryani later'. He passed on the menu to Manu. Manu said, 'Nothing right now, maybe a Veg Biryani after some time'. 'Are you eating vegetarian because of me? 'No nothing like that. Today is Thursday right, so no non-veg.' 'Idli is my favorite starter', laughed Amit. 'So, when do you like to start?' Manu replied, 'One month. That's the minimum notice period'.

Breaking the mundanity of the conversation Amit said 'Hey, your wife is very famous, Manu. I follow her Instagram. You both create nice content.' It caught Manu by surprise. Manu smiled 'Yes Amit. It's torturous. Has a husband ever survived by saying no to his wife?' Amit symbolized through his fingers sliding across his forehead to indicate as though everything is predestined. They laughed. Amit sat forward. Manu paid close attention and sensed something unknown coming his way and was all ears. 'As of now, is there anything apart from your career that you need immensely?'. 'No' said Manu.

'Good, then you please pay attention to this. The deal of this job is on only if you are ok with my condition. Because this is a position that I have newly created for you in the company. It's a position that brings with it a handsome salary, plenty of perks, commands a lot of respect, holds power, and whatnot. You are getting everything that you should be ideally getting after ten years. Think about it. Because you know the situation after COVID-19 right'. He knew that this was a precursor to perhaps a favor that Amit was expecting from Manu. Was it getting to sell the company shares to somebody, a tender, a real estate deal, or maybe a new manufacturing unit to set up? But all these were trivial tasks. They could be done with just the snap of his fingers. Why is he fretting so much? Manu couldn't quite comprehend the moment.

Amit laid down words that pierced Manu. 'I want to spend some time with your wife. That's my only condition.' There was nothing that hinted at a normal familial friendship kind of setting in Amit's words. It exposed Amit's desire of wanting to sleep with Manu's wife. Manu felt through him a sudden urge to slap Amit. He was enraged. When he got up to leave, Amit sat him down. 'See I am not those government officers who put forth cheap bargaining demands like a piece of land, money, or introductions to a celebrity. You need a favor from me. I need one from you. As simple as that. If you can't agree to this, we can't proceed with this deal. No hard feelings.' 'This asshole must have checked out my wife's profile first before finalizing my candidature'. Manu murmured to himself. It was a sickening feeling.

Amit constantly stared at Manu. There was an awkward silence. Manu realized that Amit had something else to say. There was an inexplicable vulgarity in his eyes. 'See you have a double advantage here'. Manu, although felt an immense urge to get away from that nauseous situation and text him sorry, he pretended to listen to him. 'See, my wife, will also be sleeping with you'. Amit raised his eyebrows as a confirmation of the deal and implied the righteousness of this bizarre request. 'I understand that if my wife sleeps with him I get a job, but why would I want to sleep with his wife?' Manu wondered. The waiter served Idly. Amit didn't bother about eating. Every time Amit uttered 'See' it rattled Manu. 'See if you agree to this condition and when everything goes as per plan, it's quite natural that you would carry a mountain of guilt every time your wife sleeps next to you. You might bear the burden of a big mistake, or you might feel the lack of compatibility, fuelled by someone else sleeping with her. And it could be nauseating, I agree. So, to either kill that guilt or to reduce the impact of it we are having this arrangement.'

The repugnant situation overshadowed Manu and he questioned Amit, 'Amit, don't take this personally. But is this how you have climbed up the ladder?' Amit smiled. 'Of course it's a part of our Silicon City culture right and It's called wife swapping.' Although Manu was aware of this, he never had in his wildest dreams imagined to be a part of this story. 'This has always existed, but maybe we have never had a fancy English term,' said Amit. 'Did your wife agree?' asked Manu. 'See, she remembered Sita, Sati Savitri, and all those pious mythological characters and she cried. I stopped talking to her for five days. Again, the reference to mythology; She quoted 'Husband is Divine. The wife must listen to whatever the husband Says', and I think because of this she agreed.' He cut the idly with a spoon, pricked it with a fork, and dipped it in sambar. 'See that's not the last thing right? See we are animals. You cannot control your bodily desires, especially after the first tryst with this wild experience. Now it has become an act that breaks our daily routines. Sometimes we just do it for fun.' This further infuriated Manu. 'Every individual would desire this, Manu. They might not have had the right opportunity that's all.'

Amit placed the empty plate on the side of the table and wiped his mouth. 'It might seem disgusting to Anu. So, it's not necessary that it must happen immediately. The third month after you join is fine for me. Make sure she gets pampered by the luxuries that our company provides. Let her get addicted to it. And then you propose this arrangement.' Amit gulped the remaining water in the glass, rinsed his mouth, and drank it. If at all Anu hears this, she might kill him,said Manu. 'See, believe me, you are not making a mistake. When everyone feels content, trust me there is nothing that could turn out to be wrong', He quoted as though it was a quote from one of the world's greatest philosophers. 'He put me in such a spot, this scoundrel. You might feel I have to kill him someday; Whenever you feel this.' 'Just remember this, 'He slept with my wife, I slept with his.' That's all. Every emotion would subside and seem trivial. 'A disciple of Sigmund Freud, this asshole', Manu thought to himself.

The waiter came up to the table to pick up the empty plates. Sir Order? And said, 'Sir, do you need anything? Do you need anything else apart from the two Veg Biryanis you have ordered' and looked at as though he had been an excellent waiter who remembered everything? 'No, that's about it', said Amit. Manu kept looking at the waiter and said, 'Earlier they always used to send people who never spoke Kannada. After I escalated this multiple times to the management and made a scene, they always send someone who speaks Kannada' said Manu to Amit. 'That's the right approach. You should remind everybody that walks into this city, that the city belongs to Kannadigas' he reiterated. Amit never reacted and said 'Let's go to Goa for a family vacation. After we go there, talk to Anu. If she agrees it's ok, otherwise no hard feelings. You can resign in a month from that date.' While the thought about leveraging this experience to find another job was lingering, the smoking hot Biryanis were served.

Instrutech was beyond any company that Manu could get into. The industry's best salary and amazing perks. More than Anu, Manu was enslaved to this indulgence. How you exit from a job that handsomely rewards laziness was another concern. Although he had tried his luck interviewing at other companies, it had been several months now, and he had not been successful. Nobody gave him a job. The last week of the third month was when Amit had messaged him 'Goa next week?'

Let me make the best of this trip, while Amit takes care of the entire expenses. At the end of the trip, I will reject this salacious request of his Manu thought to himself. Whenever he imagined quitting this job, he knew he would never be able to find a similar one. The act of making his wife sleep with Amit brought with it an assumption that Amit's wife would not be good-looking. But her Instagram story had surprised him. Amit's wife Pratima was more beautiful than Anu. He imagined sleeping with her for a moment and felt happy. Can he talk about the wife-swapping arrangement with Anu? How would she feel? Wouldn't she feel like killing Manu?

4

When he returned home that evening he got into a conversation 'Anu, are you interested in a honeymoon trip to Goa?' Anu replied, 'You seem to be in the mood after 8 years of marriage'. 'No nothing like that. We can't reclaim our younger years back you see. So, we need to preserve our experiences.' Manu hugged Anu who was standing in front of the mirror dressing up in a nightie and slowly zipped up the back of her dress and then unzipped it. He could not look at himself in the mirror. He kept looking at her, smiled, and kissed her neck. 'My boss Amit is also going to Goa with his wife. He will arrange everything. All four of us will bask in Goa. Am sure you and his wife will enjoy each other's company', Manu said admiring her beauty in the mirror. 'If you discuss office meetings in Goa, you will see the alternate version of me,' joked Anu. The frustration that he had about himself and Amit set up a strange enchantment that passed between them back and forth until it no longer existed, and Anu seemed to relish the fatigue after so many years.

5

Shopping for clothes was the first on the list of many things to do for a four-day Goa trip. They took the flight scheduled for Thursday. Rooms next to each other were reserved on the eighth floor of a sixteen-storied Starshine Hotel building. They met in the morning and smiled at each other. They had their breakfast. The sea in front of them looked calm while the ocean in Manu's heart carried tumultuous waves. On the first day, they preferred to skip Calangute beach which most of the Indians rather than Kannadigas preferred, and went to Baga beach, a popular destination for foreigners. They discussed the next day's itinerary and basked in the sun. Everybody drank beer. Manu saw the sunset and it strangely seemed like a metaphor for his career going down.

They came back to the hotel by around 7 PM. At the reception, Amit reiterated the arrangement. 'Today, after dinner?'. 'I cannot contain this anger, whatever is bound to happen shall happen', Manu thought to himself and replied 'Yes'. 'After dinner, let Anu come to my room and Prati shall come to yours. Let's not go anywhere,' said Amit. The thought of texting Amit and conveying implicitly that, 'Anu didn't agree' was still lingering. 'Let's meet for dinner' they said to each other and retired into their rooms. 'I am the pimp for my wife'. He uttered these words in Kannada, and it was the first time he felt words sharper than a dagger pierce his heart like none other. 'Dead I shall be trying to lay bare all of this. It is the heinous act of killing a breath called Anu who is a beautiful part of me'. The fact that he agreed to this vulgarity to advance his career was itself an unpardonable mistake he thought. That's why he wanted to confess everything to Anu and become vulnerable to every emotion of hers.

The women seemed to believe that the suave they exhibited and the fragrance they wore were the true and only indicators of their status. Dressed in red sarees, they both walked towards the restaurant indicating the pre-planned nature of things. The fatigue of visiting Goa seemed to be inexistent and overshadowed by their charm. The men were seen in their formal dresses. Amit was ogling at Anu's beauty. They had dinner while the faint music played in the restaurant.

Manu imagined confessing everything to Anu and his heart dropped. He tried hiding his anxiousness with a fake smile and got on to the lift which looked like the gateway to hell. He broke out in a cold sweat. Realizing this, Anu pushed the intended floor button on the lift. Manu looked at her and seemed to convey that everything was ok. Amit and his wife appreciated this sweet concern. When the lift arrived at their floor, both the wives retired into their rooms.

The men stopped in the corridor to execute the planned event. 'Now it's 10:45, send her at exactly 11' said Amit and walked into his room. Manu decided to not say anything to his wife, wiped his sweat stood in the corridor holding on to the railings, and started breathing slowly.

Manu saw Anu peeking out of her room, looking quite sad under the assumption that her husband was standing outside discussing office matters. While Manu walked slowly into his room he tripped. Anu ran towards him and held him in her arms. 'Is something wrong?' Manu looked into her eyes and said "No, nothing to worry' about. The hotel's mega clock ticked and indicated 11 pm. There was some noise in the background. When he turned, he saw Pratima coming out of her hotel room. Manu still wanted to send a lightning-speed message to Amit and frantically searched for his phone. 'What happened to him?' Asked Pratima to which Anu replied 'Nothing'. 'Don't worry I will take care of him' said Pratima winking her eyes. Manu froze. Anu looked Manu in his eyes slowly put Manu's hands into Pratima's and walked into Amit's room.

Anu walked in her red heels and the pointed sole cut through Manu's heart with every step. Manu could not make sense of the sexy blouse she wore and the thin thread that held everything together exposing Anu's bare back. He broke into a cold sweat, his vision blurred, and his brain went into a fuzzy mode.

■

Praveen Kumar G., a younger-generation short story writer, is a native of Bellary district. He is actively engaged in the Kannada film industry and recently directed a movie `Amara Premi Arun'. He has published a short story collection, `Yede'.

Akarsha Kamala Ramesh, translator of Praveen Kumar G Story, is a poet, translator, and short filmmaker. He has published an anthology of poems `Graphity Hoogalu'. Akarsha has translated Marcello Di Cintio's 'Pay No Heed to the Rockets: Palestine in the Present Tense' into Kannada.

6

A Bridge of Light to Darkness

Suchitra Hegade
Translated by **Fakkiresh Hallalli**

The dark streets of Kolkata's Sonagachi are lightened only after the sun has set. There is no sign of life in the cramped, dirty streets decorated with paan and khaini spit except for rows of clothes drying by day and the sound of children playing on the adjacent railway tracks. As the evening steps down, middle-aged women with heavy makeup, and shiny sarees are the first to appear. Taxis start coming and stopping by the time the elegantly made-up girls, dressed in various designs, come out into the street. In the end, the young girls who didn't even wash their faces, had disheveled hair, looked like they were in a hurry in their clothes, and sleepy eyes out of their congested rooms and stood at the door with a smile on their lips so the Sonagachi wakes up.

Strings of colored lights with Bollywood music, the sound of cesspools on both sides of the street, the scent of women's perfume, the zarda beeda in the mouths of men who are wrapped, the smell of gutka, the smell of khaini, the loud talk of drunkards all combine to create a strange atmosphere.

If Kolkata is like a living canvas, Sonagachi is a blur-like photo taken in fog;a thousand faces move but no one is familiar. Their life is simple even though the lanes of Sonagachi are tangled. A pan masala for a day, fish for dinner, girls for their physical needs. That's it!

Old Kolkata has a row of big houses. But Sonagachi has a very different shelter system. A ten-by-twelve room on three levels with a drawing room above the hub, a kitchen in the middle,and a bedroom with an attached bathroom below makes magic. Above all, the light of a faint red light bulb whirls with a fan. A small TV on the wall is the reason for breaking the silence of the room. A large mirror in the middle of the god's photos reflects the entire room. The stand below the mirror is full of cheap cosmetics like lipsticks, powder, etc. There are utensils on the middle shelf and a mini fridge that smells of fish as soon as you open the door on a high stool. Stove on another small table. There is always a bed sheet with a floral pattern on a thick bed on a couch occupying the entire room. There is a square space for bathing and washing dishes in one corner. Even if it has a screen, there is a high chance of it being rolled up in a situation where you shower three to four times a day. The old tap where the Ganga pours loudly for one hour a day as if to wash away the sins here. Buckets full of water peek out from under the couch. In the allocation of space, the Gods' photos occupy a lot of space. Along with the wall paintings, the shelves are adorned with idols of Durga, Kalimaata, garlands of flowers and lace. Like the pictures of small children in the corner of the wall, none of them match the design of the room. The world seen outside the small window curtained by an old sari is not too different.

Paro, who was sleeping on an old couch in one such room, did not come out of the room even in the evening for a week. Illnesses such as fever, cough,and dysentery came one after the other, and not only did Paro's work stop but also her savings in Usha Cooperative

Bank, which is only the saving mode for women of Sonagachi has gone empty. She had no choice but had go out that day. She sat up forcefully. She washed her face and started to make up. She feels confident enough to conquer the world as she starts to make up her face. She gently applied foundation cream to cover all her pale and black skin. She made her eyes glow by embracing the darkness within her. She put the redness of her anger stored for a long time on her lips and smiled so they started shining.

So those who saw Paro's oil-dark complexion, chubby face, red bindi, and big eyes thought she was a Bengali. People only by hearing her Hindi,say, 'She is a Madrasi…' Thus Paro is not even from Madras. But she was not the only one there, because everyone in the south was a Madrasi to them, so she stopped telling herself that she was Parvati, the daughter of Bhajiyangadi Ellappa from Soundatti in distant Karnataka. She was popularly known as Paro amongst Bengali people.

That day, Babu said in a stammering voice, "How long can you continue this way...? It will be difficult if you don't get ready soon!" Paro shivered even under the thick sheet. She had prayed to Kalima for a quite long hoping that she would never confront this situation. 'Come on still little child, go and mind your own business Babu' her words came out weakly. 'The younger the girls the better... Do you want to tell me again? All the girls born in Basti have to stand in the streets of Sonagachi one day or the other' Babu grumbled and started washing the dishes.

For the past twenty years, Paro has not stepped outside the Bad Nam streets of Sonagachi. Now and then he would go so close that she could see the Howrah Bridge and just stand staring at the attraction of that bridge. If Paro had a Majbutu bridge to connect the light to this dark life all those times... I felt that he could have held Munni's hand and sung, 'Ae Zindagi Gale Lagale'. Born as the eldest of four children, Ronavva and, Yellappa. Yellappa was an angry drunkard like Jamadagni who was running a bhaji shop in Soundatti. Paro has no sweet memories of her childhood except taking care of her younger wretched sisters. In the evening, she had to wash the bhaji pan with ash. Every day, her father used to put the pieces of leftover bhaji in her mouth one by one and caress her until her body turned blue. This still haunts her in her dreams often. She had not been to school.

During the celebration of Durga Puja here, she remembered the full moon fair of her village. It was at that fair that she met Biju, a young man from Odisha who had come to work as a laborer. Parvati being half-stomach and scorned, loved the snacks he gave her rather than his loving words. After all, she must be twelve or thirteen years old. The hunger of the stomach was more than the dream of love. After giving a packet of sweets to both of their sisters who were crying, Parvathi and Biju both boarded a lorry and came to Pune and then took a train to Kolkata. The first thing she saw when she landed in Kolkatta was Howrah Bridge standing on the Ganges. Even after passing by its beauty, she looked back again and again in the crowded streets of Kolkata, holding the hand of Biju tightly. But from the moment he stepped there, his behavior changed drastically. He carried her around and brought her to Sonagachi Street, talking to someone in Bengali, which she did not understand. By the time Parvati lost her sight, Biju had sold her to an Agarwali Mashi and fled.

Reeta Mashi, who had taken good care of her before, after she had eaten well and had her hands full, called her one day and explained that 'Dear, Sonagachhiya is a meat market... It's like there is a working girl here, golden doll'. She touched Paro with her hands.

'You have call men with your eye slash and lips tweak. They should fall in your trick.'

When Paro protested, Mashi became Kali of Kalighat. She was scared and intimidated, kept her in the room without giving her food, and brought her on the way. She snorted. The same life happened in the later days, seeing and socializing with girls of her age who came from far and wide like Bangladesh, Nepal, UP, and Bihar. She practiced the price list for minutes, hours, and rarely the whole night. She learned little of Bengali along with Hindi. She was stubborn to finish the quota for the day as soon as possible. For a few years, Paro's desire to earn money quickly and go back to the village was alive and well. The elderly women there laughed and said, 'This is the same story with the thousand women here'.

After crossing the streets of Sonagachiya, it was over. When Reeta Mashi, who thought only death was the only way to be released from there, died, all the Agrawali, Madrasi, Nepali, and Bengali girls who were with her joined her association. Meanwhile, with the help of Dalali Babu, Shotaranjan Das alias Bipa, whom Paro already knew, she rented a room of her own. It is a matter of pride for Sonagachi girls to get Babu's Dekh Bal. It's like being relieved from the work of standing on the street and calling customers in the evening. But Paro had the knack of sifting the birth of men with a glance. The newbies, the old ones, the dull ones, the ones who don't have them, the curious ones are all right... But Paro would get angry only if she saw the rarely-found bullies. Using all the words that father could not say, she used to scold her friends from the neighborhood and scold her not to step into the basti.

Paro was at the height of her day. Daughter Ellamma brought her a different life and was full of new enthusiasm. She was growing up in the mouth of those around her. Like every year, Panditji, who had come for 'Punya Mati (sacred soil)' from Sonagachi to mix with the soil of the Ganges for Durga Protima, asked for soil that year in Paro. The soil in Paro's hands, who was ecstatic, was green even without the hands of the Ganges. Sonagachi also waited like the entire Kolkata for Durga Puja. Paro earned more money in those ten days than a whole year's worth of work. It is the men called babus who do all the household chores like cooking, and washing dishes and clothes in the paros room who sleep all day, eat, drink, and get tired at night. Bipa, a servant-like man was not only cooking but also taking her daughter out in the evenings while Paro was at work. For his service, Paro used to pay for his household expenses. Some of her clients were, giving tips to her generously. Usha used to pay house rent, electricity bills, cable fees, police charges, house expenses, and the remaining money to the bank. Social workers came frequently and gave information on how to maintain their health.

Everything was going smoothly and daughter Munni was the only reason for Paro's life. Every day she begged Mother Kalito give her a good life. In Sonagachi every year Kartika Puja, which is held with more pomp than Durga Puja, used to carry Harake and dance in the procession. As in Durga Puja, she used to hold her daughter's hand and bring around all the nearby Durga Pendals. Going to Ramakrishna Mission school, Munni was feeling happy and worried at the same time seeing her growth beyond her age. The sad part is that there will be no survival after growing up. That's why many mothers left their children in the village with their relatives. A few times when Munni was bored with the environment around her, her mother came to know that her school had started a new residential school. For Paro, the thought of her daughter leaving home was distressing.

Bapi's experienced eyes began to calculate differently after noticing Paro's growth. And in the meantime, Paro was frequently falling sick now and then. Babu's impatience increased as Paro's income dwindled. Paro stares at Kali's photo in silence as Bapi, a born broker, gazes at Munni. She prays Kali not to grow up too soon.

The social workers who come repeatedly are pestering Paro to come to the clinic and get blood tests done. Now Paro is confused by looking at Munni's eyes whether she is seeking for question or an answer. Paro did not want the diagnosis of the disease that came from the fear of getting a name for the illness. She often remembers Munni's father. Nadeem, the taxi driver who first fell in love with her, always came for Paro. He loved her more than life itself. When she became pregnant when he said 'Meri Mang Bharo' to him, he removed Kalimata's vermilion and placed it on her forehead without speaking again. Paro danced as a peacock. Bapi laughed 'Idhar ka pyaar to pani ki jaise... purana behta ha to naya aata hai...' and silenced her. It is the same. After Nadeem's Nikha, his visits gradually decreased.

Paro now gets some time for himself. She just stands at the window and looks out. Basti observes the speed of life and new twists and turns with surprise. Now she is as if she has not heard Babu's interpretation of 'Behta Paani'. Men who change every night, a mind that is empty as soon as it is called into space, a body that does not match with the mind, a daughter that seems to be growing day by day... Will this race stop? She thinks in her heart that everything should not be left standing there... like Kali... like Ellamma... or at least like the Howrah Bridge, which stands undisturbed by hundreds of carriages day and night...

Paro made up her mind and stood up. She took out her cosmetics one by one. As the facial wrinkles, cracks,and spots disappeared one by one, the glow of self-confidence arose. A flash rose in the eyes that infected the forest. A large saffron lit up the forehead. The tight lip became discolored and loosened. The new saree flattered Maiya's folds. Holding Munni's hand, she crossed the lanes of Sonagachi and dropped her off at Sarada Residential School, without looking back. The Howrah Bridge looked even more beautiful in the evening light.

■

Suchitra Hegade is a native of Uttara Kannada, a coastal district. Along with writing, traveling is also her passion. Suchitra has published a travelogue, `Jagava suttuva maaye'. She also has a collection of poems to her credit, 'Ee Chitte Kadida haage'.

Fakkiresh Hallalli is an assistant professor of English and an aspiring translator. Apart from Suchitra Hegde's story, he has translated Kannada poems into English.

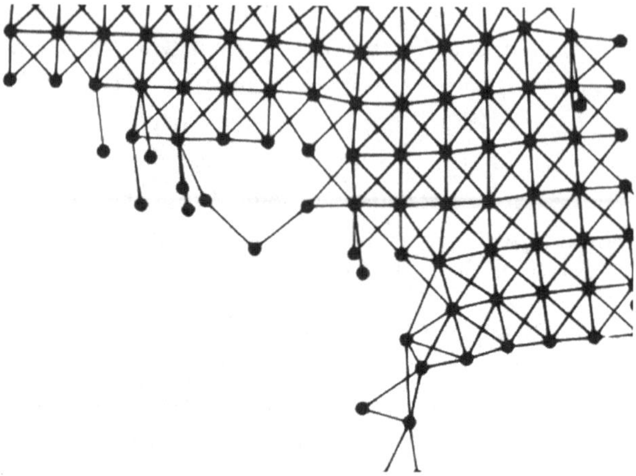

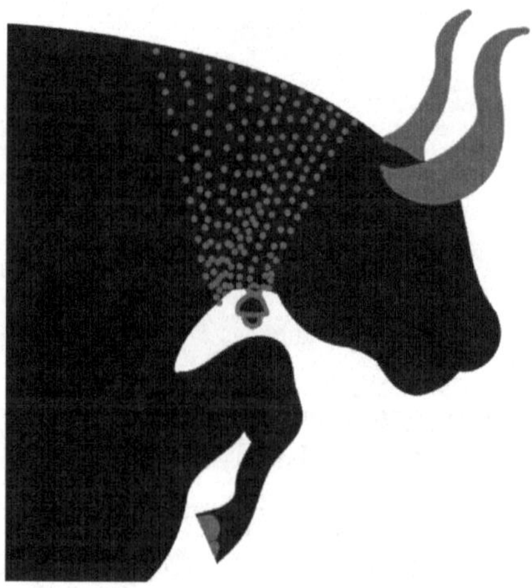

7

The Penance

Bhuvana Hiremath

Translated by **Manu Devadevan**

As twilight began to descend, the urchins rushed to the school's backyard and stood in a row with their noses running. Behind the backyard, at a call's distance, is the Dodageri reservoir. In this twilight hour, a siege of cranes played and swam, appearing to be in a caprice at the sight of flowers and buds on the lotus plants. In the last period of school, Kusumi, Vanaji, Shaili and Thanji were playing hopscotch, waiting for each other's turn. These were the only girls in class VII. There were six boys. It is a little village, some ten km from Kagineli. To begin with, there was only a single master. The school had only up to class IV. In the last two years, another master and a sister have come, and the school seems to have extended up to class VII. The village has only two buses, Krisna and Hanagallu. They come and go, twice a day. The masters come for work in the same buses.

The school bells were ringing, *ring ringring.* End of the day, perhaps? But Kusumi hadn't had her turn in the hopscotch even once. 'Your turn is the first tomorrow, come, take your bag,they'll lock the school,' said Thanji, turning to the classroom. Vanaji and Shaili also followed her. Kusumi didn't want to leave, but she had to; she followed them, carrying her bag, dragging her feet rudely, and raising dust. When they walked homeward with bags on their shoulders, those sitting on the porches in their houses made fun of the school kids. How would they keep quiet looking at Kusumi's swollen face?

'Kusumi, when're you giving us the feast? Make your dad, the chairman, spend some bucks. Enough of stacking stuff and filling the granary.'

'Have you fastened three knots on your face because your base hasn't shaken yet, my love?"

'Your father is the chairman. Vines have spread all over the holes and ditches, isn't it Thanji? Is it true that the chairman has sent a handful of parcels to your house through the postman, straight from the Krisna bus?'

'Doesn't the eyes and nose of Kusumi and Thanji look alike? See!'

'Leave it, girls. Why should we bother about village matters? If the girls tell this at home, the chairman Chandrappa the moon will turn into Soorappa the sun, my dear.'

Such was their dung head talk.

As soon as they crossed the street and entered the archway, the kids washed they legs and faces with tap water, prayed at the Basavanna temple kneeling, and took the road to their homes. Looking at Kusumi's sad face, Anasavva asked, 'Why're you making an awkward face, dear, did you meet Dad at the archway gate, did he scold you?' Kusumi didn't answer but wept bitterly. Anasavva didn't look at her any longer; she went in, placed some *karindi* chutney on the roti, and went to the courtyard saying, 'Have this, looks like you are hungry.' The cattle had returned mooing after grazing their fill at the hill and drinking water from the reservoir; she fastened them in the shed next to the house, threw some paddy stalks near their legs, and returned. Kusumi hadn't moved from her place yet. The roti in her hands wasn't spent a bit. Anasavva stared at Kusumi with fuming eyes and went in to make tea, grumbling, 'Her dad and she are both perverse alike, they sit like ghosts; get the hell out of here.' Kusumi ate the roti and went to Sister's house to study.

The Sister from the school stayed on rent near their house. She belonged to the distant Athani, and hand come here as a teacher. Her husband worked in a seeds-manufacturing company. She had a little daughter, a year or two perhaps. After school, Sister came home with a couple of kids, made tea for them, and did some household chores with them. Kusumi also joined them. Sister didn't give her any work for fear that she is the chairman's daughter. But the girl wouldn't be quiet. She would find some errands for herself. In these parts of the country, they smear the house with cow dung paste twice a week and apply what they call *kani*, a layer of red earth smeared up to the wall. There is the belief that the house looks good only if *kani* is smeared over an area four fingers wide. The old women mocked at their daughters-in-law if the *kani* lines weren't straight. 'She knows nothing, can't draw the *kani* line straight, my dear,' they told one another while sitting on the porch. Kusumi used to draw the lines neatly.

There was no work left for her today. Sister saw that she was sitting there, low in spirits; she gave her daughter a *panchami* ball sweet she had brought from home, kissed her on the forehead and asked her to give it to Kusumi. Kusumi saw the doll-like kid walking on unsteady legs, and forgetting all else as it seemed, joyfully took her in the arms and began playing with her. Then she got to some reading and writing with a smile. She asked Sister when she didn't understand something.

The Sister answered the kids even as she continued cooking. Her husband was often late in reaching home. The girls left by eight or half past eight, but the boys remained until the husband was back. Some of them slept on the porch, after having the meals there.

In the morning, it was a huge difficulty for people like Sister, who had come from other places, to go out with a mug of water to answer nature's call. Here, people got out in the dark, saying they were 'going to the water' or 'going to the reservoir,' and returned fulfilled. None of them carried a mug of water. The reservoir is spread over a ten-acre area. It lies glued to the backyard of a lane in the village on the south, the *gouton* on the east, the foothills of the hill on the north, and a dyke-like lane going to the hill on the west. Funnily enough, there was an unwritten rule in the village that consigned the women to the *gouton* banks of the reservoir and the men to the hillside. Each one washed themselves on the banks of the reservoir. In such a place, it was inevitable for Sister, a beacon of spotless light, to take Kusumi along with her and go along the dyke-like road with a plastic mug full of water and relieve herself in the eucalyptus grove on the plain-land on the hill. Kusumi woke up as usual and came to Sister's house.

They were both going to the hill. To the left of the dyke-like lane is the reservoir, to its right a low-lying hill. There were a few houses here and there, like blisters. One of them was Kusumi's friend Thanji's house. Every day while passing through the place, Kusumi raised her hand to Thanji from a call away, and both spoke with gestures of the hands. Sister walked ahead with a smile. Today, Thanji was not seen when they approached her house. A man wearing a white turban seemed to get into the house from the backyard. Kusumi was sad because she didn't meet Thanji, but she walked eating little khaki fruits and skunk vine fruits that she plucked on the way.

The school bell rang. The kids playing a variety of games rushed into the classrooms. The master who came by the Hanagallu bus, which was delayed, rushed to the headmaster's room and came to the class. He revised the lessons from the previous class and started the class VII maths of subtraction in simple equations. Kusumi, who was good with maths, asked the master a question. His answer didn't satisfy her, and he could see this. The class continued, but the discomfort over the question remained in the teacher's mind as well as Kusumi's. Now, the fragrance of the pulao cooking in the anganawadi nearby made the kids' mouths water. When the one o' clock bell rang, Thanji and Kusumi held each other's hand and rushed to the anganawadi. Dyamajji, the ayah of the anganawadi, had served in a plate each for the two; she gestured to them to eat as she served the other kids. When she made the gesture, the cyst that hung on the left side of Dyamajji's forehead moved. The two girls had their plates of pulao waiting because Thanji's mother was Sister of the anganawadi. She seemed to be from a distant country. Her name was something like Meenanjana.

Meena is what every called her, Meena. Simple and beautiful, she rarely spoke to people in the village. Thanji alone lives with her now. Nobody seemed to know a thing about her mother, father, husband, mother-in-law or father-in-law. Meena was an introvert who didn't speak much with others. Dyamajji knew a thing or two. A few people have woven whatever stories had flashed in their minds. Are they going to be quiet about a single woman? It isn't for nothing that elders of old said, that an empty pot shouldn't be kept at home, and when it is empty, it should be placed within a drum. The poor kids seem be know little. Thanji might know her past and the present in bits, but Kusumi knows nothing. She has never been to Thanji's house because her mother Anasivi had forbidden her from going. She didn't ask why, and if she did ask, the other might not have told her.

When they returned after having the pulao, Sister's class was almost drawing to a close. Her child wept, causing a nuisance; the two girls carried the child to the Basavanna temple, where they found someone rolling on the ground in penance, wearing spotless clothes. The scene made the child cry even harder. The confused kids brought the child to Karabasappa's music store, where Karabasappa placed a pack of music in the child's hands. The weeping stopped. The child was deeply fond of music.

It was the last period in the evening now. Today, it was Kusumi's turn at the hopscotch. When she was deeply lost in the game, her stomach began to pain deeply. She was telling Sister of the pain when the chairman came to the school. Why he came there is not clear. Kusumi was in deep pain and nothing came to light of his visit as he took her home.

The next day, she didn't come to Sister's house and Sister took another girl to the hill, when she saw a man in front of Thanji's house drag Thanji by both her plaits to the courtyard and beat her up black and blue, shouting, 'tell me, who bought you the earrings!' She felt that he was perhaps not the man in the turbun that she and Kusumi had seen the previous day. She couldn't stand this for long, and walked away. Yet, she felt that a man who had beaten poor Thanji so hard can't be her father. She couldn't also figure out whether the girl had done something wrong, a thought that occupied her as she reached the school on time.

Thanji and Kusumi were both absent from the school today. Upon inquiring, it was learnt that Kusumi would be made to rise on the eighteenth day of the menarche with an auspicious song, but thoughts about Thanji kept Sister worried. She couldn't hold herself back anymore, and during the loo recess went to the anganawadi, where she struck a conversation with Dyamajji and asked why Thanji's mother had not come for work today. 'Sister, theirs is a long story, you're a Sister but you're like a mother to me, leave it, I know what happened in their house this morning, Sister, poor Thanji is a scapegoat,' she said, and the cyst on her forehead moved again. This movement looked propitious at times, impropitious at other times. And for this reason, Dyamajji looked like a time-reading oracle. The day seemed to be unduly disquieting. I've come for work from afar, why should I get into these, she thought, and walked to the classroom in haste, carrying her sleepy child on her shoulders.

Anasakka had made Kusumi rest, sprinkling turmeric water on her and feeding her vermicelli and ghee. She was also lying down on a rag she had drawn near the girl. The chemistry between Anasakka and her husband, the chairman, had ended many years ago. She might have slept for an hour or two. Kusumi woke up screaming, 'snake, snake;' she was gasping for breath. Anasivi woke up, 'where's the snake,' she said, 'Mother has told me that these are times when girls have fear and anxiety, sleep peacefully, I'm here.' Kusumi reached out to her mother swiftly and held her tightly. Anasavi felt that she had been polluted, but she remained quiet looking at the daughter who was in fear. Kusumi was jabbering. The sound of jabbering was heard. When she woke up in the morning, Anasavi told Irapanna what she thought was the summary of the jabbering.

A sorcerer sat in the courtyard claiming that he'll transform the chain on Anasivi's throat into a snake; Kusumi told him that he's cheating them, for Sister had said in the classroom that all these are false; both fell into resolve and the chain with the *tali* on Anasivi's throat turned, gradually, with a mere three drops of chanted water and a bit of ash, into a large cobra, arising from the tail, and then a hood rose in place of the *tali* and bit her chest; but there was no threat to Anasivi's life, for the snake that bit her died a couple of hours later, becoming powerless, gnawing bit by bit and flowing away as water the moment it fell on Anasivi's feet. Irapanna of the book listened to the account and turned the pages of his book.

'Something good for one can be bad for another. Sometimes, the venom that does everyone bad also rises for an hour, swelling. Force exists between existence and destruction. Don't worry, be at peace. You must be contented with the food that comes your way; else you'll have to die hungry. Remember this,' he said plainly, gave some ash to be applied on Kusumi's forehead and throat, drew a yantra on a sheet of copper, made a pot, prepared a talisman chit, and placed it in Anasavi's hands, asking her to fasten it to Kusumi's arms after bathing her. She fastened the talisman chit to the edge of her sari, placed a hundred and one rupees or so in Irapanna's hands, and bowed to his feet, holding the edge of the sari. Irapanna rose and left.

Wherever the chairman was at night, he would come in the morning by teatime and have the tea she had made. Today the hour of boiling the tea was past, the time of having upma was also over, the school bell had cried *ring ring*, Irapanna was done with his book, and Kusumi had reduced and turned glowless, but the chairman was nowhere near the street leading to the house, let alone come home.

Finally, Kusumi woke up and came out partly from the dream or the illusion, ate a few morsels, and sat in low spirits. Anasavi came to the main door a couple of times, peeped into the courtyard, threw the door open, brought Kusumi to the porch, and switched on the television.

The news of Thanji's earrings didn't end there. Meena had received ten times more thrashes behind the doors than what Thanji had received in the courtyard. The people of the village had indeed spoken, each in one's way, about the wretched animal that had beaten her up. But whose words are true?

Meena had come to the village nearly ten years ago. She seems to have gone to school. It is said that she was sitting in the Durga temple on the mound by the school with her child, who was three or four years of age.

The woman who had gone to fetch water asked her of her whereabouts, and gossip began to spread across the village that she had come from a distance, that her husband had thrown her away from the house, that she overlooked her husband's words and went to a private school to work as a teacher, that her parents are from somewhere else, that she ran away after falling in love with some guy from Davanagere who had come on tour or work, that after marriage and the birth of a daughter, this difference of opinion cropped up and a quarrel broke out every day which crossed all bounds and the husband threw her out, that this woman who looks like high on self-esteem wouldn't beg anyone, that her parents wouldn't take her back, that she thought it out and reached this village where she is now. Those who heard this reproached her as they found fit.

'She spoiled one, and is here now to spoil who knows how many! O, the village's fate!'

'She should've lived holding on to the feet of the one she loved. If he throws her out, should she come away discarding him? She is simply arrogant.'

'At least for the kid's sake, can't the wretched whore hold on to the husband's feet and make a living.'

There wasn't anyone to speak against the nobleman who threw her out. This went on till midday when some sacred souls brought her home and seemed to have given her food to eat without much grumbling. The people recall even now that they were none other than Anasivi and the wives of her brothers-in-law. The mother and daughter lived by the door there, spreading out a jute rug. Thanji and Kusumi have been friends ever since. Anasivi was also kind, and looked at Meena as her young sister, giving her sugar, tea powder, and groceries in times of need. Kusumi's father, the chairman, managed to get a house sanctioned for Meena across the village and got the village panchayat's approval for appointing her as Sister in the Anganwadi. These days, all these were indeed impressive. But will the delusion of having helped someone get away from the son of a man? More so when he is the chairman of the village. That's what occurred here. Although he went again and again to Meena's house and talked of the affairs of the world, Meena didn't cooperate much. It became an obsession with the chairman to move around her house in the name of papers and signatures and more.

As the days passed, Meena also began to feel that this was a refuge for her life. The chairman used to look after her needs, from groceries to whatnot that were bought. All with the help of the village postman. The chairman's behavior began to change gradually. He stayed like a stranger during the day but began to slip into Meena's house at night like a cat burglar. Typically, one didn't think that Meena had accepted the chairman so easily. Who knows what chemistry had brought them together. Whatever it was, Anasivi's days drew to a close here. In the beginning, Anisivi was furious like a rivaling co-wife and asked where he had been the whole night. She wept and wept to a deadend. Then, it became inevitable that she remained quiet for fear of his cane. He didn't stop having his meals at home, but it was now years since he seemed to have connections or cords at home during the night. Anisivi is wasting away her life after the kids, cattle, the dung and urine of the cattle, wives of the brothers-in-law, and sisters-in-law.

On the other hand, ask if Meena is happy, and lo, the chairman who was mad after her beauty has now become a ghost-infested with suspicion. The postman and Meena are like a sister and her little brother. Chairman Chandrappa had fallen into the worst habit of looking at him or at anyone else who spoke to her for a moment with eyes red with anger, be it the master at the school in front of the Anganwadi, or the driver who delivers ration to the Anganwadi, or whatever tot of a man. Meena seems to have had thoughts of leaving the village several times. But the hawk won't let her go. The devil keeps watch like a serpent round the clock and rises up hissing. The round earth is full of despicable worms; how long could she run. If one lies fallen somewhere, she will surely be food for the worms. There's a sea of difference between running across the plains and sitting safely behind the walls with the doors shut.

Yes, this nobleman was the one who dragged Thanji and beat her up yesterday and thrashed Meena with his cane inside the house. Here's what happened:

In Dyamajji's words,

A stranger came in the Hanagallu bus, reached the Anganwadi, stood near the tank that had a water tap, and waited for Dyamajji to come to the water tap. The guy didn't even show his face clearly but walked away swiftly after giving a box of jewelry to Dyamajji who reached the water tap dripping water, asking her to give it to Thanji. Dyamajji called out to him, 'Who are you, o brother, listen,' but he walked far and far away from the village on the walking lane without listening to her. So that nobody could see him. Dyamajji thought that he was perhaps Thanji's father, maybe because he looked like one, maybe because he asked the jewelry be delivered to the girl.

He looked pretty young, so it wasn't sure if he was indeed Thanji's father. The old woman had little time to inquire; she gave away the box to Meena without so much as to look what was within, arranged the plates in which to serve pulao to the pregnant women, one over the other, and threw a cloth on her head for a cushion, on which she placed a basin.

Next, on the night when Kusumi had the dream or illusion of the snake and the jabbering, there occurred a great catastrophe. How does one describe this; the limbs shiver even now. Neither Dyamajji nor Meena knew who gave the earrings; it was too far for Thanji to know. Meena wasn't sure if it was Thanji's father although she had her doubts. The cat burglar who slipped in as usual at night from the backyard sat on the chair hissing. For the chair on the porch had reached the kitchen! Such were his ways. Did Meena get a hard thrashing when she was silently making tea? As the uproar increased, Thanji, who was sleeping on the porch rose to stand behind the bamboo door trembling, but at the venomous moment when the eyes fall on the earrings glowing on the ears, the animal ensured that it was made of gold, and turned fierce. A night passed, a day slipped away and the following night, Meena and Thanji had a rain of cinder over their heads. It was worse, crueler than cruel. At midnight, they both faced a sentence.

It was an inhuman sentence, one which no one should pronounce against another. No one should endure it either. It was a sentence harsher than the one inflicted by a demon, and not just one inflicted by one who has turned into an animal with humanity lost. The sentence was that both had to carry out the penance of rolling over the ground around the Basavanna temple five times, naked. Their mouths were tied, and they were brought along the lake to the Basavanna temple without a single tot of a human in the know. They were stripped, and they were pursued like a dog; in two rounds blood dripped from their eyes, but no light flowed into the world in the merciless night. One doesn't know if Basavanna was sitting safe and locked in the sanctum, waiting for the priest's command. The eyes of people who slip into the wretched sleep never open.

The peepal tree that spends its life taking root in the place where it stands, the shiver of the bilva tree, the buds that open their eyes on the oleander tree at daybreak, the cries of the grass that surrounds the temple—nothing opened the mortal human's eyes. What then of the stone deity? Three rounds were completed. Then four. And finally, five. The penance of rolling, the penance of rolling, Sambashiva Basava….

In the Anganwadi, Dyamajji's cyst is growing day after day like a yam, devouring time along with the time-reader. It has also stopped moving so that the sign is neither propitious nor impropitious.

■

Bhuvana Hiremath is a poet with two collections of poems to her credit. Her first collection of poems 'Trial Roomina Apsareyaru' has achieved critical appreciation. Bhuvana's another collection of poems: 'Matte Matte Martyakkiliyuttene'.

Manu Devadevan is a historian, poet, translator, and research scholar. Has published books in English and Kannada. 'A Prehistory of Hinduism' and The Early Medieval Origins of India' notable books by Manu.

8

Rumor of Crime Reporter's Report

Prakash Kugwe

Translated by **Dr. Ravikumar S. Kumbar**

He was the number one crime reporter of a reputed newspaper. All news would reach him instantly – accidents to rapes; physical assault to murders. The news would reach him even before the Police. His news sources were that unique. He was the witness of such world happenings as if accidents and crimes happened only after informing him.

He had daily conversations and transactions with the people who used to react and respond to quotidian activities by keeping all of their five senses open – the sanitation workers who begin their duties before dawn; the porters and coolies; auto-rickshaw drivers who worked day and night; gunmen surrounding the officers; security guards in front of bungalows; vegetable vendors with pushcarts; tea stall owners beside roads; and restaurant workers out of the city's periphery.

"The mistake is of that car owner Anna; he has carelessly run over the pedestrians walking on the footpath. It seems they are father and son. It's doubtful that they'll survive. They were taken in the ambulance" – thus, his sources would provide him with breaking news from the spot. They had gained such expertise that sometimes they would WhatsApp him the photos and videos. He had trained them in such a manner.

He used to help them in several ways. Hand gloves or gum boots to sanitation workers; DLs to auto drivers; promotion to gunmen- all these works would be facilitated by him or through officers. He used to give wages to porters; and tips to security guards from his pocket. He even used to provide immunity to vegetable shops, tea stalls, and restaurants from all sorts of disputes arising from anybody.

His morning cup of tea would be with the sanitation workers or porters at the tea stall. He had the company of auto drivers for a puff of a cigarette. For breakfast, he had the company of the officers who were back from their morning walks. Later on, he used to visit the SP and DC offices. There too he would first greet the gunmen and drivers before talking to the officers to exchange bits of information. For lunch, he would go to a *Khanavali* (lunch home). There he would chat with the government office staff. Some canteen was meant for his evening tea. Dinner would be fixed at a restaurant. This was his daily routine. A heap of information would pile up in front of him in all directions – from morning till night.

He used to meet prisoners in jail; speak to people admitted to hospitals with injuries; write humane reports after talking to a bike thief; a rape victim and even an orphan kid. The art of speaking and a distinct style of writing both had been mastered by him. That's precisely how he would write special reports every day to his newspaper. His byline reports would get a special place and design in the paper. He had taken care of that too. He had not just won the trust of sub editors who arranged the page and design artists but also made them his beneficiaries. He would invite them to parties frequently; their kids would get seats in a good school or college through him. He made sure that they got appointments of doctors in hospitals. If all these tactics didn't work- he used to lend them money and keep them under his debt.

"Why don't you folks get news like him?" This is how bureau chiefs of other dailies would serve notices to their reporters. This fact bothered many of his fellow reporters. They started inquiring about his news sources like detectives. After all, he was a crime reporter, right? He got the hint and fortified his news sources so that news wouldn't leak. The fellow reporters couldn't pierce through his secret sources. Moreover, his special reports didn't have any adverse effect on the distribution of other newspapers. So they kept quiet and stopped hunting for secrets.

But he was worried about a thing. Even though he filled his reports with amusement and instigations, the readers didn't respond and the distribution of the newspapers didn't bode well. Even after providing the reporter with an extra assistant, promotion, and salary hike- why was the distribution dull in the district? News editors sternly told the bureau chief to pay a visit and report back to them. Startled at this, the chief took the very first bus to meet this reporter. The crime reporter's car had already arrived to meet the chief. The car picked him up and went straight to the city's famous hotel. A specially reserved table, waiter, and supplier awaited them.

The bureau chief salivated after hearing the breakfast menu. What to eat and what not to do? He was in a dilemma. He listened to the menu again. He wasn't able to decide.

"Let's order jackfruit dosa, sir. It's the specialty here" – the crime reporter suggested to him. He too felt it apt. It was tasty and $3/4^{th}$ dosa was eaten. The chief started looking at the waiter. The reporter grasped this and ordered another plate.

"The dosa is good; it is a new taste you know," the chief said after gobbling it.

"Sir, have another plate" the reporter pleaded.

"No, it's enough for me now. I need four plates as a parcel for my family" told the chief.

"OK, Sir. What do you want next?"

The waiter came and repeated the menu.

"I had heard about *Todedevu*, the sweet dish but hadn't tasted it. Do you want a plate?" This time it was the bureau chief who asked first.

"No Sir, you please eat".

"Bring four parcels of this too along with the jackfruit dosa" the reporter ordered. The chief didn't say no. The bill arrived with the tea. Even if the finger bowl was given, the chief rushed to wash hands near the sink. The reporter picked up the bill. He hadn't paid the bill yet, then – "*Che…che…*. Why did you pay? I would've paid" – the chief uttered.

"How can you pay the bill while visiting my city sir?"

Both laughed sheepishly. The car started again; both didn't know towards which destination. In the post-prandial ecstasy, the chief had forgotten the reason for his visit.

"Sir, did the completion of yesterday's edition get delayed?" The reporter himself tried to make the chief memorize.

"That's Mangalagowri's daily mistake. To return home early, she completes the page even before the deadline. She either skips the news which comes late or else fits them somewhere. The news of a son killing his father had been put in a corner. I scolded her and changed it. The deadline finished then. I must serve her a notice".

"Poor thing sir, her husband works in another city. She alone has to take care of the disabled son. Just warn once, that's enough" explained the crime reporter.

This didn't go well with the chief. He felt uncomfortable. For some moments he thought that the matter was drifting to some other direction . . .

"I've saved you from notice; I need a party" – the reporter had already texted her. She had replied with an emoji of thumbs up, folded wrists, and a heart.

The chief asked "Even if we've provided your district with a permanent sub-editor and a page designer, why isn't the circulation improving?" The news editor demanded clarification.

"Whose job is circulation sir? We people in the editorial section cover all the news. We provide special reports daily; what else is needed, sir? The circulation section must do promotion activities everywhere. But the representative isn't up to the mark; if you change him the problem could be solved"- the reporter complained.

"Indeed, circulation is not our job; there's no problem concerning the news"- the chief thought to himself. "What you tell is right; I must meet that circulation representative once".

"Why should you meet him? That too isn't our task sir. The circulation manager is in the bureau, ask him only sir".

"That's true", the chief got angry at the news editor. "He sent me here unnecessarily"- the chief scolded him in his mind and added – "Anyhow I've come here. I'll meet him surely; ask him to come".

The reporter called the representative in doubt. But the representative picked up his phone call on a single ring. The meeting was scheduled at the crime reporter's usual hangout – the tea stall in the city circle. The car sped up. It left the main road and began traveling on service roads.

"It's your luck that he's available for a meeting today sir. It's Friday na? By this time, he would've been ready to go to his village. He doesn't work at all; he's always waiting to go home"

"Is he married?" the chief questioned.

"Yes, he is. His wife goes to work outside. He's got a daughter. But this chap never skips visiting them every single week"- the talk revolved around the representative. He had arrived before the car reached the spot. Mutual greetings were exchanged.

"Why didn't you come today morning, Anna?" as the tea shop owner asked him, the chief was introduced to him by the reporter. The chief started inquiring about the representative while eating *bhajji* with tea. The crime reporter pretended to be on a phone call and had moved a bit further away from them.

"What's the issue here?" the chief asked the representative.

"There are a lot of problems here sir. I can't tell you here. If you accompany me to the field I could explain"- the representative replied calmly.

"Why should I go the field with him?" thought the chief but didn't tell him. Sternly he said thus- "Field visit can wait; but why are you not selling the newspaper even if you are provided with exciting news daily? This is a serious issue. I've to report to the news editor. Tell me properly".

"I told you already sir; there are myriad problems. Come to field visit"- the representative didn't loosen his grip.

The reporter's phone call was still on; the chief got infuriated and shouted at him.

He came hurriedly and said, "It's the editor's phone call; he wants to ask the SP not to file an FIR on the car accident that his son was involved in when he visited this city".

Raising his eyebrows, the chief said "Oh! Is it?" and further informed him "He's inviting us to the field visit. Let's go".

The reporter joined them hesitatingly.

All the three got into the car. It stopped in front of a middle-class house at the old periphery of the city.

The chief objected –"You called me for a field visit, but have brought me to somebody's house".

Not even the presence of a single soul even after the gate was opened ajar by them. Dusty tiles; disheveled verandah; drop silence and the shadow of the deceased.

After a while, an octogenarian Ajji came out querying- "Who's that?"

The representative answered, "We're from the newspaper. Professor's home? We wanted to meet him".

Ajji became serious. She looked at the triad from head to toe. Thought for some time – "Yes he's inside the *Pooja* room, I'll call him; be seated".

Both the reporter and the chief questioned the representative- "Who are these people? What's their connection to our paper?"

"He's a professor; we had carried a story in our paper". As the representative murmured the reporter got alert. He remembered his special report written under the heading '*Prof-lecturer Lovie-Dovie*'. That was written based on the tea shop owner's news. The *chai-wala* had reported him after eavesdropping on the lecturer's gossip at his stall.

"After the news appeared in the paper, that lady lecturer quit the college. This Professor's wife committed suicide. He's seeking psychotherapy after becoming detached due to sorrow. The little son was bereft of his mom. Now this Ajji is feeding both her son and grandson" – the representative reported quickly.

The professor came out with folded hands to greet the triad. Everybody was introduced. He asked the reason for their visit.

The agent said – "You're an old reader of our newspaper. But since last month you have discontinued our paper's subscription and are buying a new one." He further added, "We got to know that you've spoken ill of our paper. That's why we came".

"I don't want to discuss that; you can leave"- the professor got up from his chair. The triad looked at one another. After regaining his balance, the chief said "Don't feel bad sir. Tell us what happened?"

"I said no already"- the professor reiterated. "You spoilt my whole life. I was her PhD guide. It's common for us to sit together, discuss, and travel together. How do you decide that if a man and woman are together it is love-sex? In what ancient era are you living? Did anyone complain about us? Is there an FIR filed? After all, how did you write the report in your paper that too in a filthy language? Does it suit your paper? My colleagues had spread the rumor to stop my promotion. Is it right to report this?" The professor was fuming in anger.

Both the representative and the chief turned towards the crime reporter.

"I was told that it was credible news . . . That's why" – the reporter hadn't finished his sentence.

"What sort of a reporter are you? Just because I do not visit his tea stall, he has spread such rumors against me. You've reported that by trusting it!"- scolding in singular the professor went inside but rushed out at the same speed. Before the screams of *'Haa. Ayyo'* he stabbed the reporter with a knife. The chief had already sprinted past the gate. The representative came in between and took away the knife in the professor's hand. Even while trembling, the professor was moving towards the reporter menacingly. The reporter sled and fell in the chair. His shirt was blood-soaked. Ajji created a ruckus and took her son inside. The representative picked up the reporter slowly and took him to the hospital in the car.

Breaking news spread- **Mentally unstable Professor attacks a journalist.**

The media personnel visited the hospital in teams. Quick treatment was arranged. The doctors declared that there was no danger to his life. After informing the editor, the chief asked for the contact number of the reporter's family to inform them.

"Whose number shall I give? Even at 40 years of age, he's unmarried. His father is in the village; his mother is dead. They have an area nut farm. After his mom's death, his dad had married another woman. His connection to his village is weak. Even if we call his dad he wouldn't come hastily" – said the reporter and became pensive; his eyes welled up.

The chief began hurrying to get back by claiming duty hours. As the crowd increased in the hospital, he left without telling anyone. He didn't forget to take the food parcel along. As the representative was busy nursing the reporter, the fellow journalists were getting ready to protest against the attack.

■

Prakash Kugwe, a journalist for decades, has engaged in social and environmental movements in the Western Ghats.

Ravikumar Kumbar, an assistant professor at Davangere University, has actively engaged in translations from Kannada into English. .

9

Danube-Volga-Ganga

Salim Nadaf

Translated by **Naveen Halemane**

Fiona called from Frankfurt.

"Hey, Doc… There is an engineer on international deputation in Yagadalpur. He wants to return to his homeland; his company is asking for a doctor to accompany him on his journey. Is there somebody who could drop him to his country?", she said with a deep German-accented English.

"Which country? City? What are his ailments?" I asked.

"Vienna… Austrian… sixty-three-year-old engineer, has the symptoms of paralysis. His CT and all are normal but he is feeling severe giddiness, he can't walk on his own. Could you please drop him to Vienna, please?" She pleaded.

"Where is he staying, presently?"

"I may not be able to utter the name like an Indian… something called Yagadaalapur… Chatis garha…" I googled the names while she was trying hard to pronounce. Yagadaalpur was Jagadalpur and Chatis garha was Chattisgadh. What business could a European old man have in a notorious Naxal area? I felt a bit puzzled.

"Fiona, he is in Jagadalpur. I will go through his medical details. My European visa is still active. I will go with him myself. You check the flights."

"Yagadalpur to Vienna…" she repeated. I interrupted, "It is Jagadalpura... in your country, English 'j' is pronounced as 'ya'. But here J for Jagadalpur." I thought about yogi-jogi, yugala-jugalbandi and imagined how she could utter jaya jaya.

She brought me to present by saying, "Oh yeah, Jhagadalpore??"

"Which flight do you prefer? Emirates? Etihad? Lufthansa? If it is Lufthansa, you have transit in Frankfurt, others in the Middle East…" she said.

"Not Lufthansa. They serve pork. Book in Emirates. Transit in Dubai… Meals is good. Bengaluru to Jagadalpura, from there to Delhi, then Dubai and to Vienna by the last flight." I spoke.

"I will arrange everything and email our Delhi office. Stay in Delhi for one day and meet the neurologist." She replied.

"Yes, I know Dr. Mishra. He would do the needful quickly."

"As of now, the physician in Jagadalpur has said he is fit to fly. But when you ask for a wheelchair at the airport, the Emirates might ask for the medical details. You have three days. You just fill out the Emirates Medical Form. I'll request for a quick permission for your journey," said Fiona.

"Ya, the patient is not on external oxygen. So, we might get the permission readily." I ended the call and filled out the medical permission letter for the Emirates journey.

I pondered about the clothes, footwear, and emergency medicines for a five-day journey. I Bought Maggie cup noodles and a packet of Besan Laddu at the Reliance Mart and headed home.

Our executive from the Delhi office called on my cell and said "Doc, flight tickets have arrived. Up and down business class tickets are confirmed… the media form you filled is submitted to Emirates and it is approved too. Not communicating with the patient. I will call him and need to get his consent. I will call through a recorded line and will put you on call." She called me back within a couple of minutes and said "Doc, the patient didn't take my call... I'll try again. By the way, how much do you want for your expenditure?"

"I've 100 Euros at home… get me 300 more. Would you please send it to my home?"

"It's already Friday evening. Tomorrow is Saturday. Forex and all would be closed… I will inform you at the Ebix currency exchange at Delhi airport. You would be given cash there. You have a Bengaluru to Raipur flight at seven-thirty in the morning. Sorry, there is no business class in this sector. You can go from Raipur to Jagadalpur by Innova and come back by the same vehicle to Raipur, then to Delhi. Raipur-Delhi is also economy class. Sorry about that. Please manage yourself." She ended the call and sent the tickets by email. I flew to the capital city of the new state of Chhattisgarh.

Before the lockdown, I had brought a patient to Austria, his condition was quite serious. I had treated him for eighteen hours continuously. The patient who was two years younger than me had a strange wound to his limb and suffering from pain. We traveled from Delhi to Graz via Munich.

In Delhi, he had said very humbly, "See I know Hindi, I love India… theek hai koyi baat nahi". But while having an injection at the Munich business lounge, he began to show his anger. As soon as he reached the middle of Europe, he began to change colors. By the time he reached the hospital at Graz he was completely changed. At the Graz hospital, he had shaken the whole hospital with his loud shout about his admission getting delayed. I could see racism in his behavior in the way he was teasing me in broken English and his grumbling in German. A senior doctor said, "This gentleman has brought you safely from Delhi. Instead of being grateful, you are showing your anger for a delayed admission. Don't you know the admission procedure here? Your company has not informed you about your arrival here. Your wound is not a fatal one. Mind your behavior! Remember that this is a hospital." Then only he calmed down and apologized deeply before sending me off. But, by the time I returned to India, he had sent big mail with a series of lies. I tried clarifying for a whole week and finally declared in one sentence that he had a mental illness and got full marks for that. I recalled all that now. The patient in hand now is sixty-three years old. I felt he would surely be sensible and he might not have the European ego. I slid into the soulful celebration of completing my nine years in the areal physician's profession and entering the tenth year.

A 63-year-old could have BP, but diabetes is scarce among Europeans. If the CT scan is normal, what could be his problem? Could be TIA, which plays hide and seek with the blood circulation to the brain, or could be simple BPPV which can cause giddiness. If it seems like a serious illness, he could be admitted to the hospital in Delhi and I could return to Bengaluru. Had Poha served by the air hostess and slid to sleep. As soon as the flight landed, I got a call,

"I'm Shatrughna, your cab driver. I'm in the VIP lane. You could see an ambulance before me. If you have heavy luggage, I'll come to assist you. Please call back, sir." I ended the call and came out. Shatrughna welcomed me while keeping my trolley bag with the medical kit in his Innova Crysta.

"Are there Naxals in the area we are going?" I asked.

"No sir. It is still further. Sukma area of Andhra border. It has rained very much here. We could visit Chitrakoota Waterfalls and move on." He said, springing his vehicle on the road. By the time we had Potato Bun for breakfast and reached Chitrakoota, it was already past noon. After half an hour's picnic, the vehicle had directly reached Jagadalapura. In the city which seemed smaller than Belgaum, it was not difficult to find the patient. In the muddy lane, showed up my patient with a walker, waving with his trembling hands, "Hi, Doctor". I felt relieved as I saw him. "Welcome. I'm Harold Lobischler. I came out with this walker lest you get angry. Otherwise, I walk without any support. I had severe diarrhea for three days. From continuous dehydration, I began to feel giddiness. Even after diarrhea and dehydration were cured my giddiness didn't stop. The local doctor did the CT and it was normal. My BP got quite high. I was given tablets for that as well as for giddiness. Even now, feeling a little giddiness," he said with a laugh, making tapping sounds with his Hawaiian slippers while he sat on the sofa.

"Mr. Harold, this is good news for me. Come, let me check your BP. Nevertheless, use a wheelchair till you reach home. Your safety procedures can be completed quickly in all the airports. Our journey starts tomorrow morning at eight. Tomorrow's dinner in Delhi. The day after tomorrow afternoon, MRI and consultation with Dr. Mishra. By the way, your BP is too low. Stop your tablets. I've checked your CT report. Let's have the neurologist's opinion tomorrow. Let's reach Delhi first."

By now, Harold was feeling sad,

"I've roamed around the whole world. But I had never lost my heart in any situation. But this time… somehow, I am scared. I long to reach my home more intensely than ever. I'm in a great hurry to see the faces of my wife and daughter." He sobbed.

"I'm extremely sorry for your condition, Mr. Harold. Ten thousand kilometers away from home, anybody would feel equally scared. Don't worry. I'll take you home safely. You're in safe hands now. Put a signature in this consent letter. If you don't understand any word or sentence, please ask me." I said, putting the consent letter before him.

"I don't have any doubt about your company. There couldn't be any word that can't be understood." He said, signing the papers right away.

"Get your things ready. We are departing from here at eight tomorrow. Remember to stop your BP tablet. Your passport, visa, and medical reports would be in my custody till you reach home safely…" I spoke. In the dhaba, we had lunch. I reached my hotel and it was six by the time I woke up. Did little exercise, had a heavy breakfast, and sat in the car. "Ten minutes to eight… I'm ready…" said Harold over the phone in an enthusiastic voice.

"I'm just there. Let your luggage be out" I said, and stopped in front of Harold's house.

"Doc, this old man is my colleague, a chemical engineer. He is German, I am Austrian and my mother tongue is German… Ha ha…" he said introducing a six-feet bald European who stood there. I shook hands.

"Take good care of my friend, doc," he said. I nodded assertively.

"This is Shuklaji. Our site manager. He took great care of me," he wiped his tears hugging a short person.

"Come. Let's have a pre-journey checkup." When I did a general checkup, his BP was a little high. Maybe because of the excitement and anxiety of going to my homeland, I felt. I sat him in the vehicle and fastened his seat belt. We headed towards Raipur from Jagadalpur. Harold was very cheerful. I didn't want to talk about his illness and bother him. Decided to discuss the relaxing and lighter things.

"Mr. Harold, tell me about you and your profession. I don't want your personal and confidential matters." I spoke.

"Ya, I am a mechanical engineer. We are presently building an iron production unit of the National Mining Development Corporation. In that, my job is to construct a furnace that separates iron from its ore. In simple words, I am building a huge kitchen. Ha ha ha… Construction work is almost over. When the plant begins to work, we will come to know its quality. The furnace is 99% ready. When it begins to work its constructor is very much needed. In the beginning, a lot of fine tunings are required. Therefore, though all my work is completed, I am returning with a feeling of incompletion," he said sadly.

"Your illness is not that serious. You can return after a couple of days' rest," I said.

"Thanks, doctor. I love India so much. Probably, I never felt so relaxed in any other continent or country. See, for a person like me who has spent his whole life in ore and mines, I am extremely proud of ancient Indian metallurgy. While the ancient Indians were pioneers in metallurgy, the rest were still like stone-age people. I have studied the Bhagavad Gita as well, I keep reading it occasionally. That's my favorite book. "

"What is your origin? For example, like Vikings, there should be a name for your community too, right?" I said.

"Didn't get you… see, my and your retina are of the same color, which means somewhere our origins meet." I was surprised.

"I must investigate this. But Hitler had sent his followers to India in search of Aryan pure blood."

"Oh! I didn't know about it, I have to do some research on this."

I showed a picture in BBC News on my cell and said, "See here, the team in this picture had come to Tibet. This Nazi officer was in charge of this Search for Aryan mission."

"Hey! this is Heinrich Himmler. Hitler's close associate… This is curious. I understand your question now. I don't know my origin. I am a pure Austrian. Like India, for the mineral wealth, there were too many invasions on Austria by the neighboring Romans. They were often doing so for the quality of iron ore. Since the war was an important part of life, they needed iron for making swords, knives, and shields." He seemed like a treasure. I asked,

"Are you a Roman, by any chance?"

"Impossible. I am a pure Austrian, son of a local farmer; my ancestors were all local farmers. Italy was our neighboring country. There have been a lot of battles for the mines. Since you asked, now I suspect my wife is a Roman," he laughed.

"After a married life of forty years, you are curious about her lineage," I laughed.

"Not like that… my wife is a great beauty. Every man, woman, or child who looks at her gets attracted to her. When I had taken her to Korea, one of my local colleagues was attracted to her, and tried to be friends with her, he had brought two tickets for a movie and stood before me. 'You? With my wife? Give me the tickets. I will go with her.' I snatched the tickets and went to a movie with her. He was very much humiliated and sent a bar dancer behind me. He made her provoke me and took some photos in sexy poses and showed them to my wife. She didn't care at all. She was very proud and confident about me. By seeing my wife's physical beauty, now, I'm curious to learn about her ancestors," he said proudly.

"Yes, I too like to learn about you and your wife's ancestors. As you said earlier, the color of our retinae are same… Then it'd be like a union of Ganga and Danube rivers." I laughed. He looked at me with surprise.

"Danube!? … oh, your knowledge of geography is awesome… like the Indus River, the Danube too has a rich heritage. It is the biggest river in the whole of Europe. I had my childhood and youthful days there… and I want to spend my old age there. There I would die too. I have recurring thoughts of death these days, you see. The body which cycled through the length and breadth of Jagadalpur, when it begins to lose its balance and trembles, I feel I'm in an extended old age losing its balance like the death is hovering around."

"I think we should not go back to the matter of disease. We were talking about the Danube River", I reminded Harold, "See, a hint of death brings a lot of changes in the personality. In a jiff, one could have a negative personality. Get me a dosa in the Mukdee Restaurant ahead, I like Shutney. *Dosa* is one of my favorite food items in India." he said.

"It's not shutney, it's chutney. If you are praising North Indian dosa itself like this, I'm imagining what would happen if you taste South Indian dosa and chutney"

"Is it? I've spent seven years in North India only... for some time in Bhilai. Lot of bondage between me and Iron... Ha ha ha..."

"Sir, Mukdee in one hour," Shtrughna said.

"Thanks, sir... I can wait for one hour... Doc, I'll pay the Mukdee bill" said Harold cheerfully, I agreed.

"Austria is a German-speaking country, how are you connected to Germany? Don't you have your Austrian language?" I asked.

During Hitler's rule, Austria was a part of Germany. See, Hitler belonged to Austria, he wanted to become an artist and sought admission to an art school, but admission was denied there. You know the story thereafter. "

"Oh! Is it? Hitler should have become an artist." I sighed.

"Before becoming the dictator of Germany, Hitler who was an Austrian, won the hearts of the people. One of my uncles was in Hitler's army, an ardent fan. Even after Hitler passed away he would greet everyone with 'Hail Hitler' only. He didn't believe the defeat and death of Hitler till his last breath... Hail Hitler! ha ha ha" he laughed raising his hand.

"What else did your uncle say? See the personality of Hitler. He had a great influence on his soldiers" I said enthusiastically.

"Ya... Nobody knew the plans of Hitler... When he started constructing roads, the unhappy people, understood its significance during world war..."

I cut him short by saying, "Autobahn... Autobahn... Right?"

He looked at me seriously and said "How easily you remember the cryptic names of history!"

"I'm a history freak, while writing about Aryans, I had read about Hitler."

"Then, I'm traveling with a writer-physician. I can generally tell a few things. My wife's family was quite academic. There were many books in my home library of the Nazi period, but I didn't read them. I got busy making children with a beautiful wife. Then, for my international profession, I spent more time in Asia. My wife had two girl children and brought them up. I roamed around, drank, and danced in different nations. Here and there had the same affairs with women, these days, when I look back I doubt if I'm a womanizer or I slept with stranger women in a drunken state?" He said with shaking lips. I thought of breaking the seriousness,

"Where are your children?"

"Yeah, my elder daughter is beautiful like her mother, a tramp like me, has studied something and stays in Hong Kong now. When she was in Hong Kong, I was in China, I had a girlfriend there too. Though, at this age, I didn't need a girlfriend for sex, I used to sleep with that Chinese. Fascinated by my daughter's beauty, a rich boy fell behind her and got married... They all had come to our country to see her. Their travel and staying charges, oops! In return, they too had invited us to Hong Kong and threw a grand party. Now my daughter is a Chinese daughter-in-law and Hong Kong citizen. With an excuse to meet her, I used to go to Hong Kong from here and then fly to China, have a good time with my girlfriend, and return. Now my China friend is not well and is a little worried. I'm feeling guilty."

"What does your daughter do?"

"O she works for an Italian fashion brand in Hong Kong. Sometimes, she comes to Italy, sneaks into Vienna, and meets her mother. Earns a lot. Another daughter is married at my place only. Has a child. Happy with what she has. Not ambitious like her elder sister. "

"And your wife's profession?"

"As I told you she is beautiful and people get very much attracted towards her. She was a saleswoman at a gift shop. Due to her, the business was going great in that shop. But she got bored of the sales job and quit it. She did a psychology course and now she is a counselor." He told proudly. I noticed that he repeatedly praised his wife's beauty, and wanted to ask if he feels she too has some affairs, but kept mum thinking it would be offensive.

"See, my daughter is learning to surf in Hong Kong," he said showing me a video on her mobile.

She was in a bikini and didn't seem very beautiful. Thought how much he could have trusted me to show his half-naked daughter's video. Though he had left his country, his soul had been revolving around his wife and daughters, but I felt sorry for his girlfriends.

"See, we are at Mukdee Restaurant. Hold my hand. This traveling by car has increased my giddiness. Let's have dosa first then to the loo." I assisted him and made him sit in the AC room of the hotel and ordered for dosa.

I said, "Harold, your company has paid for the travel. I'll pay all your food expenses"

"Oh, is it? Fine. I don't want to put you in a fix by breaking the professional formalities."

"Forgot to ask you, how far is your home from Vienna airport?"

"Only two hundred kilometers."

I was shocked.

"Don't worry. Ours is a highway, European vehicles would reach us home within two hours."

"Since I need to come back to Vienna, I asked. My hotel is in Vienna. A journey of four hours... Nearly six hours..." By then Harold had finished his dosa. I got him to urinate and then sat him in the vehicle.

"You stirred strange memories in me, doctor," he said looking at me. He raised his hands,

"Es steht ein Soldat am Wolgastrand

Hält Wache für sein Vaterland."

I was startled along with Shatrughna as he began to sing louder like a European opera singer.

"Doc, this German song is very special for me, my uncle, the same Hitler's soldier, used to sing this. I learned to sing along with him. I slid into my childhood, because of you. He taught me this song, saying, Hail Hitler. On YouTube, you just watch Ivan Rebroff singing this Wolgalied song. He puts us to tears." The bearded singer's song on YouTube began to echo in our Innova.

"A German soldier in The Battle of Stalingrad sings this song in despair. It's a pathos song seeking the help of God as he trembles with hunger, cold, and without ammunition."

"Why does the German soldier sing, that too in Russia?"

"Hitler fought with Russia to win Stalingrad. Had he won Stalingrad, he would have gotten oil wells of Azerbaijan and Baku of the Caucasus region. Since Stalingrad was industrialized, Hitler thought it would be advantageous to win Stalingrad, and attacked Stalingrad. It is on the banks of the Volga River. So, the desperate German soldier sings this pathetic song, Volga lied, standing on the banks of Volga."

"Oh, interesting! Go on with your story of Stalingrad." I asked

"Hitler thought he could win over Russia just as he had defeated France, and attacked Stalingrad. But it was a foolish idea. Russian cold weather, untrained new German soldiers, lack of food and ammunition, the Battle of Stalingrad incurred a great loss for the distant Germany. The soldiers faced depression due to the defeat. Though scared in the beginning, the Russian army defeated the Germans with clever battle tricks. Then, an anonymous soldier sings this song in despair. Both sides suffered a lot. With the Battle of Stalingrad began Hitler's downfall. Then Nikita Khrushchev changed the name of Stalingrad to Volgograd. Now, the Germans are supporting Ukraine and building hostility with Russia. History repeats." he said. I sighed and said, "Wow, great history. There could be many details with your Hail Hitler uncle. We shall discuss this in the flight". We boarded the Delhi flight in the Raipur airport. Our discussion didn't continue on the flight. As soon as we landed, a message about the appointment with Dr. Mishra had arrived on Harold's mobile.

" Doc, the girls at your office are very able. The neurology appointment is fixed for tomorrow afternoon. Afraid that the local doctors might cancel my flight journey."

"Just now you have done a flying. Don't worry. We are flying to Europe tomorrow." He was still worried. Stalingrad and his uncles were all haunting him. He overcame them and when we reached the hotel, he said,

"I shall have a beer and go to sleep"

"Harold, drinking is prohibited till the end of your journey. Alcohol can increase your imbalance. The next day Harold stood shivering before Dr. Mishra, who said there was no need for an MRI and asked to stop BP tablets told me to take him to his country soon and conduct all types of tests there. In big letters, he wrote, "FIT TO FLY". We reached Delhi airport. All the formalities were finished within half an hour and we reached the Emirates business lounge, when he said, "For the first time I completed security and emigration". He was very eager to board the Dubai flight. His uncle was dancing in his head saying "Hail Hitler! Hail Hitler!". In the Emirates business class, didn't talk loudly and got down at Dubai. When we were waiting for the Vienna flight at the Dubai business lounge, his BP and pulse were checked and when we reported the stability to the office, we came to know that the patient's company had arranged an ambulance to Vienna to directly take him to the hospital. There was no need for me to go to Harold's place. Travel started showing its effect on the third day. He made a video call to his girlfriend in China and introduced me to her. I didn't like the talk with his immoral girlfriend. I greeted the Chinese short girl and withdrew from the call. Harold could feel my displeasure and stayed mum. While waiting for luggage at Vienna airport, he came nearer to me,

"Doc, how shall I express my joy? You have intense curiosity towards my uncle. He was there during our wedding. He had some books and articles from those days. The current government has banned Nazi books and literature. Though Hitler is dead and hit the dust, my uncle died saying Hail Hitler! I, who belong to his family, I traveled the whole world, earned a lot, and had illicit relations with women wherever possible. Though my wife was beautiful and stayed without me for months together, she did not tread the wrong path. She brought my both daughters up. She made my house, a home. She didn't destroy it. Now, for the past week, when death is lingering around, my evil deeds are haunting me. I have cheated on my wife for so long. For the rest of my life, I would stay loyal to her. If I confess about my adultery in foreign lands, she might die in shock. I love her intensely. I will stay with her in the last days. I pay my penance by serving her. This is my confession before you. No more talk and discussion on illicit relations. I thank you immensely for helping me reach my country alive. Doc, I thought I was dying." He started crying while hugging me. He cried a lot too.

"Here, an Indian gift for your beautiful wife." I handed over a small packet.

"Oh, so nice. My wife loves Indian sweets a lot. When I got down, felt guilty that couldn't bring any sweets for the poor lady. She loves *Besan Laddu*. Thank you for the sweets and for bringing me to my country alive." He said while wiping his sweat. He sat on the ambulance chair and hugged the sweet box with his both hands.

■

Dr. Saleem Nadaf is a practicing doctor and short story writer. He has published an English novel, 'The White Discharge: Private Stories of a Government Doctor', in recent years.

Dr. Naveen Halemani is a lecturer by profession and has engaged in translations from Kannada to English.

10

Keelya

Praveen Kumar Honnakuduri
Translated by **Rishikesh Bahadur Desai**

It seemed as if the whole town smelt of death. It was a macabre evening of sad songs, flowers and wreaths, and the annoying sound of crackers. All the roads in the town led to the burial ground.

The name of the town was something else, but the villagers called it Kvati Gudi, or a `fort temple'.

It seemed as if the collective grief was entering the narrow lanes of the Kvati Gudi.

The Body

Women were busy washing the streets that seemed to thirsting for water. They lamented among themselves, that only the good pass away soon. There is an old saying in these villages: `Even a corpse feels the burden of debt'. True to the saying, some slackers were busy playing cards in the nearby temple. These are the guys who had never seen the dead man's face. Some other kind souls were carrying the body, though their shoulders ached. There were not many to share their burden.

However, they were signaling to passersby to come and take over. But there were not many to exchange shoulders.

Some relatives were talking among themselves endlessly, as they had met after a long time. ``Such are the woes of kinship. When they are far away, they will fight without facing each other. But when they come face to face, they will talk build castles in the air, and then bring them down". This was one of those momentary thoughts in the drought of words.

It was Ganachari, standing at a distance who was waving to everyone. He sounded as if he was yelling: ``Put down the corpse at the junction of these three roads and pour some water in its mouth for the last time."

And that is what everyone did- pour sesame water into the mouth of the dead.

This watering can be a wonder, I tell you. Everyone lined up and poured a little water, one by one. Though the mouth had a putrid smell that put them off, they covered their noses and went ahead with the ritual. The water was not just that. It was water mixed with sesame seeds in an earthen pot. They took `Darbe', a few strains of straw bound together, dipped it into the water, and sprinkled it into the body's mouth.

There was a bag tied near the head of the body that I found very attractive. I scrambled to get a closer look at it. But I could not find a place as everyone was rushing to pour water. They pushed each other and moved forward. I was excited to know what was inside. I got a glimpse when I moved a little closer. I saw the tiny grains, they were so slender, as if invisible to the naked eye!

Someone untied the bag tied near the head and threw it away. Usually, the three-road junction would have signaled the end of the road. It meant that the graveyard was here. The body would be brought down to the ground, and cremated. The bag of foxtail millet was untied, and thrown away after a brief ritual.

Ganachari asked the hearse bearers to stop and to turn around. No one seemed to oppose his commands. As he said, those who carried it in the front were to change their places with those who were carrying it in the back. That is because it was the last lap. Ganachari put the half-boiled rice on the soil as if to sanctify the dead body by driving away evil spirits.

I felt cringed, looking at him perform some rituals with the body. With the blink of an eye, he signaled to everyone to move away. Ganachari began his work in his usual style.

The body on the hearse was of a very popular leader. He was the Gram Panchayat member of the village. The Ganachari and others were acting as if the body was ageless, though the organs like eyes and ears were not. His body was decorated and carried further for some distance.

The Dead Member

Everyone knew that the politician who lived a life of lust had no children, but it was not discussed in public. There were so many people in the crowd, but none to express sympathies with the ill-fated woman. Their sympathies were only for the public to see. Just as a rich man arranges artifacts in a showcase. They would all act as if they lent a shoulder for the poor woman to cry on, only to move on. There was none to stick with her to provide her moral support and protect her, like a large shady tree, in a hot Sun.

The widow probably knew that this was momentary condolence. She moved closer to her husband's ear breathed nonchalantly and sighed. The body did not respond. She rested her head on the hearse and heaved a painful breath.

The woman in the group gathered around her and wrapped her with another saree, saying this was a gift from her maternal home. It seems sad to see that even in a house of mourning, rituals rule.

She was dragging her weary leg as if she were carrying the weight of the earth. Her legs were weak as there was no end to her moaning. She was still very young and her youth seemed to be basking in the sun. Emptiness filled her eyes. The grand procession before her eyes seemed meaningless. She had lived a life darker than death.

The graveyard was at the last turn on the road out of the village. Interestingly, the Gram Panchayat member who had just died had got this burial ground sanctioned by the village.

The graveyard was still 3-4 miles away. The hearse bearers were tired and weak. The heavy burden of the body seemed to be circling them like a weary night watchman going on around the house.

Earlier the town did not have a graveyard and people burnt their dead on the banks of the town stream. It was all okay when the stream dried. But during monsoon months, it was very hard to dispose of the bodies. You could not burn them due to the rain and you could not bury them as the bodies did not dry up even after 2-3 days.

This monsoon was no different. Corpses did not decompose for days. The stink of the bodies got mixed in the petrichor to create a new smell that was unrecognizable.

Once there were such heavy rains that it was difficult to spot the Sun. Few people ventured into the streets. The cold streets were missing footsteps. Shops and shanties were closed for a few days. They prayed to God for customers. But they could not find any. They had all put up posters in their shops equating customers to God. Darkness had killed the light all around. But there was no evidence of that. Even priests who were found loitering around were hard to find. They sat home as if they would be polluted if they set foot outside. They cursed the rain and waited for normalcy to return.

They reached the gates of the graveyard. They came to a stop. No one needed to carry the hearse any further. Everything ended here.

It seemed even the Gods were feeling the cold but for a different reason. The silk shawls they had been draped in were sweating from head to toe. All the wanders- dogs, cats, cows, and he and she buffalo had gathered under the roof of the temple. It was their empire.

The Hero of The Town

Keelya, however, was not put off by the stinking smell. He was too accustomed to the stink. He was equally unresponsive to the pleasures of the petrichor during rains or the disgust of decaying corpses.

What was ironic that there were few people to carry the dead body of the man who was hugely popular in the town when alive. The body was lying in repose for enough number of people to carry it.

The damp walls were waiting to collapse. Ants popping out of the crevices of the walls were lining up one behind another, like a police parade. The rains had turned villagers into Olympians. They were competing against each other in jumping over potholes filled with water. They were not doing it for medals, but out of fear of slipping in muddy waters.

Whenever there was a death in a family, Keelya emerged as the head of the family. No one needed to tell him about the final rites. He had a sidekick, called `Member'. His real name was Lakshmana. He was no member of the Gram Panchayat, but his undying ambition to be a member, had everyone call him by that name. These two were the heroes of the village, during their deaths.

The so-called `Member', who was in his 50s, had never won an election despite fighting several times.

But he was not the one to lose hope. His hopes of winning an election were flagging their wings. But then, he was the only known associate of Keelya. If he did not turn up, then Keelya did not attend any cremation. At the most, he would prepare a pit and stand afar.

Just then, the hearse carriers circled the pit three times and lowered the corpse.

The Other Member

Keelya and his sidekick member were humble folks without ego. They saw God even in the dead. They never let an egotistic person anywhere near them. After all, people with the biggest egos became ones with dirt under their hands. He took down the shroud and placed it in the pit.

The task of decorating the burial site, the dull, deadening job was given to Keelya and the members. But they had toiled for hours to make it look rich. It was as though the cadaver was treated to all the riches that the man had not enjoyed when alive. The others were engaged in their routine. With the body placed in the hollow, they closed its face with a face cloth. The face of the body was as white as the cloth. The cloth is meant to temporarily mask the body so that those standing on the ground do not see those in the pit. I came to know about it very recently.

They stripped the clothes off the body and re-arranged it to face east. They began kneading the soil around the body. They would smear the body with the soil later.

Sometimes, when they removed some topsoil, they found some bones or skulls. Keelya knew that the termites found on the site were hungry. They got attached to the hands and feet. He was delicate even to the worms. He smiled while thinking: ``When alive, they belong to others. But when dead, they are mine".

People covered the complete body with the softened soil. Now, no one could see it was naked.

As this was the last time everyone would see its faces, they kept the face uncovered. The body was made to sit in a seated pose like a sage on penance.

Ganachari, the priest, had the privilege of sitting on the dead man's scalp. He was applying vibhuti to some copper plates. Member

Lakshmana. The member would take them and place them on the left foot, right foot, left shoulder, right shoulder, scalp, and stomach. Then he would proceed to tear the Mangal Sutra of the dead man's wife.

Ganachari removes one or two gold pieces from the chain and gives them to Lakshmana asking him to put them in the dead body' mouth. But the member does not do it. He seldom puts gold in the mouth of the dead. That gold was later sold in Marawadi Shiva Seth's shop. Both of them shared the money equally.

Once this was done incognito, they removed the cloth covering the face. After removing this, there was another pooja. The rites nearly ended. Attendees slowly began to go home.

Keelya was standing near the gate of the cremation ground and was getting some papers signed by the Kvatigudi elders.

On one side of the paper, there was something scribbled and on the other side, he was getting everyone's signature. No one was asking Keelya what it was but they were just signing anyway.

The `white' paper was so dirty with traces of soil and dirt that no public office would treat it as a document. Keelya still had enough energy left to run around. I see all this and wonder. It seems there are so many confusing questions, that I could not find any answers.

Keelya must have applied hundreds of times to the Gram Panchayat for a house under the BPL nomad quota, but he got nothing. Simply because there was no proof that he was from this town.

His name was omitted somehow. Even the now-dead member used to tease him. Those words evoked laughter. Now he is gone and Keelya is conducting his final rites, silently.

The low evening sun was sinking as if calculating the height to which he had risen. No one stays here permanently, you know.

The graveyard was nearly empty but for the locals, who leave only after the customary Earth Worship.

The Pooja means shaping the soil in the form of a dome and the Ganachari standing on it.

All should pour water on their feet and offer to God, Dakshine, or some change from their pockets. The Ganachari took away the Dakshine and broke the coconut while chanting the Mangalarati mantras.

Now, all walk out without looking back. They leave for the town without talking to each other.

Outsiders rush to catch their bus. The full graveyard became empty as the evening came on.

I wanted to spend some time in the graveyard. Spending time in this cemetery is a kind of intoxication. It adapts well to the hardships of being single. Nothing is complete here. It is all just half-half, like this man sitting here.

I sat on the stump of an old tree shaped like a bench and looked around. Everything seems new every time I see it.

These logs must feel they are not new to this cemetery. In burning the body, they have burnt themselves. The wet soil has turned dry due to the blazing Sun, black beads of the broken Mangal Sutra, broken bangles, and flowers that smell nice, even though they are fading. The cloth covering the body, the broken pot from which the rice gruel is oozing out.

They were all looking at the clouds. They did not look at me. Birds on branches were not singing. They were waiting for us to leave so that they could eat up the left over rice. Shadow of the mighty banyan fell on the leaky hut of Keelya, which was deserted most of the time.

Bharati

Outside the graveyard, there was a woman at a distance that I could see clearly. Still very young, she looked like she was taking a bath with her saree on. As she got closer to the gate of the graveyard, it became clear that she was Bharati.

This puny little Bharti lives on the streets of Kwatigudi. Every road in Kwatigudi knows her footprints. Bathing in the open is nothing new for her. Her saree is stuck to her body. She keeps her body covered with turmeric. She tends to rub turmeric on her red cheeks, face, legs, and hands.

She would pick a flower that someone had worn, put it in her flowing hair, and let it blow in the wind. She used to apply turmeric to her natural pink-coloured skin and pamper it every day. Half of the saree covered her face while the other half swept the floor while she walked. She walked gently as if she sailed. I have seen Bharati living in Kwatigudi for a long time. There were no known relatives. She looked like a girl of marriageable age.

But she seemed abnormally upset. She acted as if she was always scolding someone or crying. Once she began crying, it went on for days. Many small boys are afraid to see her. Mothers used her name to make their children fall asleep.

She had a daily routine of walking twice a day in the streets as if to relieve herself from that pain.

No one knew what she underwent. The ground seemed silent as she walked. Her soiled bag seemed to have collected dirt from all around the village. In that bag were a couple of burnt steel utensils, a half-broken spoon, a lump of rice in a plastic sheet, a lump of rice, money bag, coconut oil, a can of saffron, and a couple of sarees given by women of Kvatigudi.

Even though Bharathi bathed only once a week, washed her clothes, or combed her hair, she decked herself up like a bride. She applied turmeric all over her body. If any woman stopped her, she would burst out crying, as if cursing herself. The whole town fell silent as she spent the whole day crying without anyone bothering her. The story in Kvatigudi is that she pelted stones at elders of the town who tried to talk to her. They were left with bloodied heads and noses.

She speaks very little. It seemed as if she answered her questions. She squandered her youth in the dusty streets of town. Thin as a lath, she roamed the streets begging. She sought grains but never cooked food. Every evening at five o'clock, after she collected alms, she walked to the public tap outside the cemetery. She took out a pot and washed it while abusing some invisible villains. She had chosen a specific place outside the graveyard.

Her hut was very much like Keelya's. It had no door. It was half open to the sky, but she felt no cold breeze. In the ground beside the hut, she made a hearth, piling a few stones around.

Some days stray dogs and pigs roamed inside her hut. She cursed the mongrels, and the pigs, but made no effort to shoo them away. She kept cleaning the grain, and the stove and began cooking.

She applied a coat of mud outside the pot so that the rice did not burn quickly.

She always kept a long bar of firewood. She took it to the place where they burnt the corpses. She pulled out some burning coal pieces. She used them to light a fire. At times, she picked half-burnt logs from the pyre and used them to cook rice. In her eyes, these logs were potent to burn the whole world down. She smiled at that thought. The fire seemed to have a character of its own. It danced to its tunes and then died down suddenly.

Looking at it with a bright face and with no worries about the world, she looked at the burning rice, the burning pyre, and the compound. Staring at the sky, she warmed herself to the fire. Mindfulness of the pyre, and looking at the rice boiling on the stove, she pushed the logs into the stove with her left hand. Once the rice is ready, she takes it down. She goes to the faucet to wash her hands and feet. She puts only the rice on a plate and starts her meal. She spent several nights in the burial ground, all by herself.

She always ate boiled rice. Never with any spice or curry. I have seen her do this so many times.

It is just bland rice. She kept the leftover rice in the open. Sometimes a dog at it. Or else, she ate the same rice for breakfast and started her daily routine. Everything seemed a wonder. It was neither temporary nor complete.

The Hut

I came home in the evening after the rites. I began thinking of Bharti, who was bathing with a sari on. But this night was different. I could not sleep at all. I just rolled around the bed.

Sometimes I was bored with the city, sometimes with my work. While spending the day in this town, I used to dream of my village and head back for a few days. Lately, there was not much interest in my work. The boredom of the town was constant.

I had lost my father and his love. I thought of my slacker brother and rushed to my native village often.

This time, while riding back from home, there was a loud song being played. Thinking there might be the annual car fest for Shravana, I began looking at my mobile phone. The bus is reaching the graveyard. Usually, I took the seat next to the window, so that I could look at the graveyard.

I tend to count the bodies or burnt logs and deduce the fall in population. But now, everything seems new.

The dark cemetery seems bright. This is the enemy of darkness. Time marches on along.

The town seems quiet. But there is a ceremonial public shelter in the cemetery. Mango leaves hung across and turmeric water was everywhere.

Countless legs moving across the still graveyard, foreheads full of saffron, bangles in hands, marks of turmeric on some hands, beedis in the hands of some youth, their mouths filled with smoke.

A speaker tied to the gate was loudly screaming out songs.

A few people were walking in front of Keelya's house. It is not a house built by devouring the ground. There was neither a window to let in the light inside, nor a proper door to welcome visitors. Keelya himself built this structure he called home.

It was just a tiny hut. But seemingly beautified today.

The cemetery was almost deserted except for a few people loitering around. The lone Neem tree swung its branches and leaves in the air as if it was gasping for breath. The rows of lights strung on the Neem tree were blinking as if they competed with the few stars that are visible during daylight.

The smell of cooking wafted around the cemetery, filled with smoke from the burning bodies.

Usually, a home hosting a wedding is a scene of celebration. The young boys and girls create a new world. But there were no young men in this wedding home. The cemetery, which seemed to be in a mess, can now be seen from a distance and can be recognized from the house.

Seeing from afar, sitting in the bus, I immediately spotted Keelya. His whole body was painted in turmeric. He was sitting inside the cemetery.

He was a shortish guy, around five feet tall. Not very fat. He had no bulging stomach. No obese legs or hands. He looked five or six years younger than his actual age. Smeared with turmeric, his face was shining. He looked even younger and brighter.

He walked out of the graveyard. The surroundings fell silent. His turmeric-painted body seemed to add another challenge to the several questions and the ensuing silence.

But without going on any such quest, he was at peace. He held a beedi with his middle fingers and exhaled smoke. His face was calm. His breathing was normal. There was no change in him.

Only the clothes had changed.

■

Praveen Kumar Honnakuduri is a younger-generation short story writer. Trying to explore writing narratives in a local dialect.